WEST HIGHLAND WALKS: ONE

HAMISH MacINNES
WEST HIGHLAND WALKS: ONE
BEN LUI TO THE FALLS OF GLOMACH

"Pleasure is the outcome of exercise."
Motto of Clan MacInnes

HODDER AND STOUGHTON
LONDON SYDNEY AUCKLAND TORONTO

Acknowledgements
Photographs by Hamish MacInnes. Photographic artwork by Graeme
Hunter.

British Library Cataloguing in Publication Data

MacInnes, Hamish
  West Highland walks
  1 : Ben Lui to the falls of Glomach
  1. Highlands (Scotland)–Description and
  travel–Guide-books
  I. Title
  914.11′804858   DA880.H7

ISBN-0-340-35971-4

Contents

Introduction	7
Tyndrum for Ben Lui	16
Rannoch Moor and the old drove road to Glencoe	20
Buachaille Etive Mor and Glencoe: a cirque of mountains and bloodshed	31
Ballachulish to Castle Stalker	74
Kinlochleven to Fort William by the military road; and by Loch Eilde Mor to Glen Nevis	84
Fort William and Inverlochy Castle	92
Ben Nevis	97
Glen Spean, Glen Roy and the Road to the Isles	109
Ardgour: Glen Tarbert and the Rough Mountain	113
Into Morvern: the rough road to Loch Teacuis and Ardtornish's dark fortress	119
Sunart and Ardnamurchan: the Bay of Spaniards and the Great Eucrite	128
Moidart: the Young Pretender and the funeral road to Dalelia	145
Arisaig and Morar: Prince Charles Edward, Morag and Mallaig	159
No roads to Knoydart	171
Glenfinnan, Loch Arkaig, Glen Dessary	179
The Small Isles: Canna, Rhum, Eigg and Muck	193
The Great Glen and ways west: the Battle of the Shirts and the Loch Ness Monster	209
Kintail: Eilean Donnan, the Five Sisters and the Falls of Glomach	223
Glenelg: Iron Age brochs and the road to Skye	237
Gaelic and Norse Glossary	246
Index	250

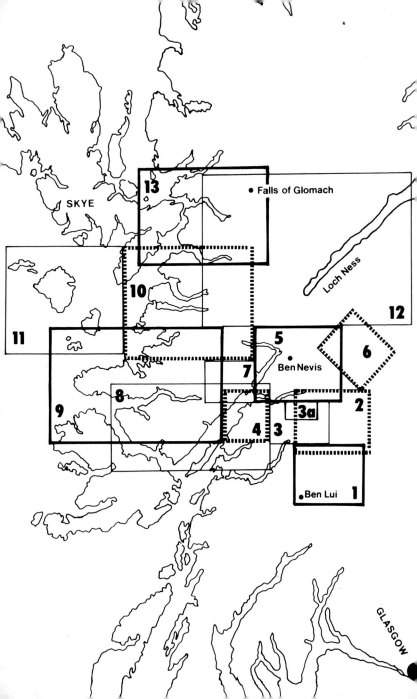

Introduction

IT HAS BEEN a longstanding ambition of mine to produce a book on the Highlands which would reflect a little of how I see this rugged, windswept land. I am indebted for the years of sheer pleasure which these lochs, mountains and moorlands have given me; their solitude and the fascination of their history. In time one begins to assemble the jigsaw complexities of clan feuds and the pattern of life which evolved from the desolate glens. Glens made increasingly desolate by the Clearances when sheep replaced families, and Highlanders, who had tilled their land and tended their beasts for centuries, were themselves herded like animals, driven to the shores to make way for sheep and told to "fish or die". From 1763–75, twenty thousand people left for America alone; the majority of these were voluntary emigrants from the Highlands and Islands.

I have tried to portray with my camera the many and varied moods of the Western Highlands, including also the places of greatest historical interest. But my attempt must inevitably fall short of the ideal and I hope that readers will feel inclined to go and see for themselves; in so doing they will be amply rewarded.

Had I shared the view of Henry Ford who said "History is bunk", I should not have written anything at all. But, out of consideration for his and similar opinions, I have kept the text concise and appreciate that many historical gaps must be spanned by the discerning reader, for whom there is fortunately a wide choice of literature.

Some people (obviously English) state that the two most consistent factors in the Scottish Highlands are the rain and the midges: true perhaps, at least for the midsummer visitor. Spring and autumn are usually the best and driest months to holiday in Scotland, spring being the most favoured season, for though

there may be snow on the tops in May, it comple-
ments the freshness of the glens and the sharpness of
the air often gives desert-like clarity.

The area covered by this book lies between the
Sound of Mull in the south and Kyle of Lochalsh,
venturing into the interior of Scotland only at Loch
Ness. The text and photographs follow a progression
from Tyndrum and the Moor of Rannoch northwards,
taking generally the most convenient roads to reach
the various places of interest. The selective visitor
can choose any one part of a region which takes his or
her fancy. To get to know Scotland, roads and cars
should be left behind. Indeed I sometimes find a
vehicle can be a positive hindrance in some of the more
out of the way places; it is often much easier to continue on foot, than to return to a car.

Although there is no law of trespass in Scotland,
and many of the old tracks are rights of way, it is
better to ask permission before venturing over the
hills and through the glens, especially during the
stalking season which starts in September on most
estates. But it is worth noting that land under the
benevolent care of the National Trust for Scotland is
not subject to any restrictions at such times.

In compiling this book I have attempted to cater for
all degrees of energy expenditure, from the leisurely
prospect of viewing a castle which entails a five-
minute stroll from one's car, to long and strenuous
walks into remote but rewarding recesses of the
Western Highlands. Where possible I have included
variations to walks which will enable a change of plan
should the weather deteriorate and, with a bit of
judicious map study on the part of the walker, other
alternatives will become apparent. Having been fortu-
nate enough to see the region covered in this
book over a period of years in all sorts of weather, I
have tried to present a balanced coverage of places of
historical interest, together with walks in areas of

scenic beauty. Beauty however is in the eye of the be-holder and perhaps not many readers would agree with me when I say that the Rannoch Moor has a peculiar fascination in a winter's blizzard or that the naked rock of Sutherland adopts a fresh charm in rain and mist.

Included in the text are some walks for the younger at heart which include overnighting, either in a tent or in a bothy, but the majority of the walks can be done in a day, or part of a day. Fortunately or un-fortunately, depending on the way you look at it, some of the walks don't end at the same point as you started from. This may cause complications but I feel that this can add that bit of zest to the day's adventure and, after all, it would no longer be the wilds of Scotland if there was a shuttle service between lonely Highland glens.

As I have spent a considerable part of my career rescuing people from the hills and mountains of Scotland, I cannot stress too strongly the need for readers to take care on these moors and hills. The maps in this book show the routes of the walks described, but they are meant only for general placing reference, and walkers taking the longer hikes into secluded parts or mountainous areas should take more detailed maps with them as well. Sudden adverse weather may necessitate a change of plan, and here also a more detailed map of a wider area becomes an essential, as does a compass and, still more important, the ability to use both correctly.

The West Coast presents a complicated, loch-in-dented coastline, rather like a frayed cloth. The hills are relatively low, but they are also exposed to the wide Atlantic: wind and storm can blow up very quickly indeed, occasionally even bringing snow to the higher tops in summer. When venturing on to the mountains, be prepared with adequate clothing, a map, compass and spare food. The spring snow can linger into summer in north-facing corries and there are often frosts at this time of year. The snow surface can become very hard and correspondingly treacherous to the unwary. Therefore always choose your route according to prevailing conditions and the speed of the party. Since this book caters for such a wide age and fitness group, I have omitted any reference to time in respect of the various walks. As long as enough daylight is allowed for the return trip, without being too tired, any one of the expeditions should be safely within the capabilities of the average walker.

The central region of the West Highlands is crammed with history. In the distant past Mesolithic people, including the flint users who emigrated from Ireland to the Scottish mainland, moved northwards through this area, but left little evidence of their simple way of life. It was probably the Neolithic tribes, who succeeded them, who constructed the chambered cairns. They were a race of seafarers who came up the West Coast from the Mediterranean. The vitrified forts were built much later, during the Iron Age. Their pattern of distribution suggests that enemies approached from the east; the brochs, too, were of this period and were probably a development of the dun or fort. Brochs are only found in the north and west of Scotland; they are circular with very thick walls, sometimes up to 40ft (12m) high, through which run galleries. Typically, the only entrance was a low, narrow doorway. Brochs were possibly built as refuges against sea-raiders, or in defence against the "Fort People" from the east.

The Picts first appear in history at the tail end of the third century AD. There are records of them fighting the Romans; so persistent was their harassment, that the effective influence of the Roman Empire was pushed back to the Forth-Clyde boundary; later it receded even further south to Hadrian's Wall.

Scots moved over from Ireland in increasing numbers early in the sixth century. They were a Gaelic speaking people who brought Christianity with them. In 563 Columba founded the Celtic Church which flourished for five centuries and, from his base in Iona, commenced the conversion of the Picts, travelling as far as the Pictish capital at Inverness to convert King Brude.

A great struggle ensued between the Picts and the Scots, the latter being ultimately victorious, and in 843 Kenneth MacAlpin became the first King of Scotland. With the passage of time, and partly due to the influence of David I (1123–53), a division again became apparent in Scotland. He introduced feudalism by making grants of land, especially up the eastern coastal plain and along the Moray Firth. The Celtic, Gaelic speaking people of the north and west bitterly opposed this Anglicisation, with the result that the geographical boundaries of the Highland Celt commenced with the mountains and embraced the Highland regions of Scotland. Here they developed as a separate people with their own language and culture, living under a totally different structure of society: the clan system. It was a family union, where the members were united under a chief, and each tribe or clan bore the same name.

The Norsemen came in a series of invasions and dominated the western seaboard for four centuries, but by the mid-thirteenth century the Scots had overrun the Viking colony of North Scotland and had occupied the Hebrides. The Vikings were finally defeated at the Battle of Largs in 1263, but they have left their mark in the placenames and culture of the Highlands.

The centuries following were times of anarchy. The Western Highlands were little influenced by the wars to the south – even the War of Independence in which starred the indomitable Bruce. But it was an era of bloody deeds in the lawless Highlands: of repeated massacres and reprisals. A verse which holds more than a grain of truth tells that after God made the Highlander from horse droppings . . .

> Quoth God to the Highlander, "What will you now?"
> "I will go to the Lowland, Lord, and there steal a cow" . . .

After the fall of the Stewarts and the upsurge of Jacobitism, the Highlands again became ensnared in the web of Scottish politics. Clans had merged for mutual protection, giving birth to such powerful confederations as that of the MacDonalds under one supreme chief who, from about 1354, took the title of the Lord of the Isles.

Both James III and James IV did much to subjugate the unruly clansmen. Between 1493 and 1499 James IV sailed to Western Scotland six times and many Highlanders fought for him at Flodden; he had a smattering of the Gaelic which enhanced his popularity with the clansmen. The Campbells, under the Earls and later the Dukes of Argyll, always associated themselves with the protestant Lowlands; inevitably, they became a hated and feared clan.

Despite the troubles, an oral culture survived and even prospered. Each chief had his bard who recorded events in song and verse. The bagpipe became the versatile instrument of both war and peace. During the seventeenth century and the early part of the eighteenth, the Highland scene was relatively peaceful and during this period lived some of the greatest poets: Duncan Ban MacIntyre, Alexander Macdonald, and Rob Donn.

From time to time there were abortive attempts to win back the throne for the Stewarts, but the one with the most far-reaching effects proved to be the Jacobite rising of 1745, which changed the course of Highland history, bequeathing an aftermath of misery and depredation. It now seems incredible that the adventurer, Prince Charles, could have rallied the clans as he did, arriving from France without money or arms, with a surplus only of confidence. What the young Prince lacked in pistols and louis d'or, he made up for in eloquence and personality. One is forced to admire his audacity and regret his final decline in exiled defeat: he eventually died an alcoholic. Prince Charles's trail whilst fleeing from Cumberland's troops after his defeat at Culloden, zig-zags through the following pages like an historical meteor.

The punitive measures employed against the Highlanders after the 'Forty-five were crushing indeed. Men loyal to the Crown fared little better than those with Jacobite sympathies. Wearing of Highland dress was prohibited and the penalty for simply playing the pipes could be transportation. The chiefs were deprived of all authority over their clans, whilst the Disarming Act forbade the carrying of weapons by the clansmen. Gaelic speech, too, was discouraged. These acts above all caused the disintegration of the clans. Some of the laws were not rescinded for thirty years; others not at all.

The chiefs became lairds. There was a boom in cattle, so many of the chiefs either sold or leased their land to the highest bidder. The old way of life was totally disrupted and emigration increased. Then a series of famines occurred between 1768 and 1773: crops failed and the cattle died. The destitute people, clothed only in sacking, scoured the beaches for edible shellfish.

Later the cattle trade declined and, in the late eighteenth century, it was realised that sheep were able to weather the Highland winter and provide an alternative. This discovery marked the beginning of the Clearances; people were thrown out of their houses, many of which were subsequently burned, and forced to move to the coast or emigrate. The sheep needed space . . . On one occasion a shipload of Camerons arrived in Sydney and a man, scanning the passenger list, was heard to exclaim, "Look here, the Camerons will soon be filling the country. Over two hundred of them have arrived on this one ship!"

People often wonder why the Highlanders accepted the Clearances so humbly – there was very little bloodshed. This was mainly due to the fact that the menfolk were away fighting in the Napoleonic Wars and the clergy, who wielded a powerful influence over the people, ignobly supported the lairds. But the Clearances were economically inevitable.

The decline in the Highlander's traditional way of life had a drastic effect on his outlook. The most enterprising travelled overseas; those who stayed were not helped by the rigid discipline of religion and suffered severe hardships. The numerous men who were evicted to the coast built hovels, fished and tried to raise crops without any security of tenure. They were at the mercy of the factors and the land-owners, with no legal redress since the lairds were also the magistrates. At this time, in the late nineteenth century, dissatisfaction was growing. Deer forests and grouse moors had become fashionable for the rich and in some areas crofters were forbidden to repair leaking roofs with rushes or heather because the removal of the raw material might cause the grouse discomfort! Crops were eaten and trampled by marauding deer; but deer, to the common crofter, were untouchable.

The tinder was set alight at Braes in Skye when irate women forced police to burn an eviction notice. But the law returned, spurred on by an enraged Inverness magistrate. Sixty police under two sheriffs and officers arrived at Braes, close to Portree. The Battle of the Braes was fought with batons and stones.

No lives were lost but a battered police posse limped back to Portree. Gladstone, who was Prime Minister at the time, was concerned. Warships were sent to the island and troops landed, but the population of Braes was unimpressed. Following this incident the Government at last realised the injustices which the Highlanders were enduring; the result was the Crofters Holding Act, 1886, which gave the crofters security of tenure. Nowadays the croft is too small a unit to be commercially viable and crofters usually hold another job as well. Inevitably the young people move into the cities, seeking work, and the proportion of the elderly increases each year in crofting communities.

The discovery of oil has for the present given a fresh lease of life to the Highlands, and several new industries have been created; some, alas, accompanied by pollution. It is time people realised that Scotland's greatest heritage lies in its unspoiled scenery: seemingly unproductive wild tracts of country are its most valuable asset. Over the years the Highlands have scarcely altered; Glen Sligachan is probably the same now as when a tired Prince Charlie squelched through its bogs in 1746. Let us hope that in the future this unique land will not be exploited beyond retrieval, but allowed to remain essentially a "Wilderness" area within our nation.

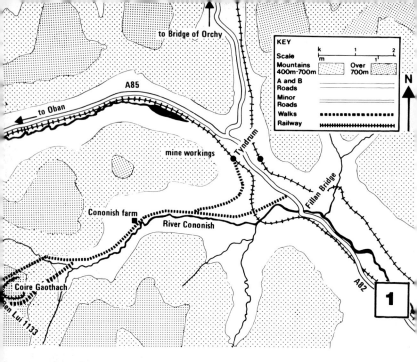

KEY

Scale			
Mountains 400m-700m		Over 700m	
A and B Roads			
Minor Roads			
Walks			
Railway			

to Bridge of Orchy

A85

to Oban

mine workings

Tyndrum

Fillan Bridge

Cononish farm

River Cononish

A82

Coire Gaothach

Ben Lui 1133

N

1

Tyndrum for Ben Lui

FOR ME THE Western Highlands start with the long climb towards the Bridge of Orchy from the fork of the main road at Tyndrum. From here to Cape Wrath is a kaleidoscope of moor and glen, of mountain and torrent; ever changing, always fascinating and a joy to explore. Ben Lui (3,798ft/1,113m) is the highlight of the approach to the village of Tyndrum, and is seen here to its best advantage at the head of the wide strath of Cononish, on the left as you head north on the A82. If you feel an urge to climb it, a forestry road leads off close to Tyndrum Lower station (for this insignificant village boasts of two stations). From here it skirts across the hillside to join up with the

Ben Lui, near Tyndrum. The summit in early spring. ▶

old road which follows the River Cononish. This track offers an alternative start, leaving the main road a short way past the bridge on the A82 which spans the River Fillan.

The track continues on past Cononish farm and grows tired as it reaches the head of the glen. Here you are under the great north-east corrie of the mountain, Coire Gaothach. A sporting route to the top, without any great difficulty (provided the hard winter snow has gone) takes the left-hand edge of the corrie and affords some gentle scrambling en route. A different descent can be made by taking the ridge to the right, cutting back down to the corrie floor at the easiest point.

Some easier hours can be enjoyed in picking over the talus at the old mines, where interesting samples of galena can still be found. The workings are close to the main road fork, on the hillside to the south-west.

Beinn Dorain (3,524ft/1,074m) is the prodigious mountainous pile on the right as one approaches Bridge of Orchy. This was a favourite haunt of one of the greatest Gaelic poets, Duncan Ban MacIntyre. He was a dedicated hunter, yet also loved the deer. In his most famous poem, "The Praise of Ben Dorain", he writes of the hind:

> Volatile, vigilant, there
> One with the horizon she goes
> Where horizons horizons disclose.
> Or lies like a star hidden away
> By the broad light of day.
> Earth has nothing to match her.

Duncan Ban MacIntyre was born at Inveroran which lies on the narrow road leading to Forest Lodge from Bridge of Orchy. From Forest Lodge a track heads west to Glen Kinglass through some of the finest

◀ Ben Lui, Tyndrum.

scenery in Argyll. The path passes Loch Dochard to arrive on the eastern shore of Loch Etive. Here a less luxurious track continues to the head of Loch Etive. If transport can be arranged in Glen Etive, this offers a superb walk of some twenty-six miles through the Black Mount.

Rannoch Moor
and the old drove road to Glencoe

FROM FOREST LODGE the old Glencoe road can still be walked for eight miles to emerge on the new road, the A82, close to Kingshouse Hotel. This is also a three-star excursion but not nearly so energetic. To the west, Stob Ghabhar and her big sisters Clach Leathad and Meall a' Bhuiridh are poised on the lip of the Rannoch Moor, which extends to the right like a lunar landscape. The Rannoch Moor is an area of desolate splendour, probably seen to best advantage in early morning, when mists cling to the lochs, or in winter under a blanket of snow with red deer treading its fastness. At one time it was a great reservoir of ice, fed by glaciers from the surrounding peaks. The ice spilled over to escape westwards through Glencoe and Glen Etive; eastwards along the lines of the lochs – Rannoch, Dunalastair and Tummel; and northwards through the defile where Loch Ericht now nestles. Later the Moor was covered by a great forest – part of the forest of Caledon which extended as far as Braemar and Loch Affric, probably as recently as Roman times. An inspection of the peat, which is twenty feet thick in places, reveals gnarled tree roots. Part of the old Black Wood of Rannoch can still be seen close to Ba cottage by those who walk the stretch of military road, between Forest Lodge on Loch

Blackrock cottage on the old road to Forest Lodge. ▶

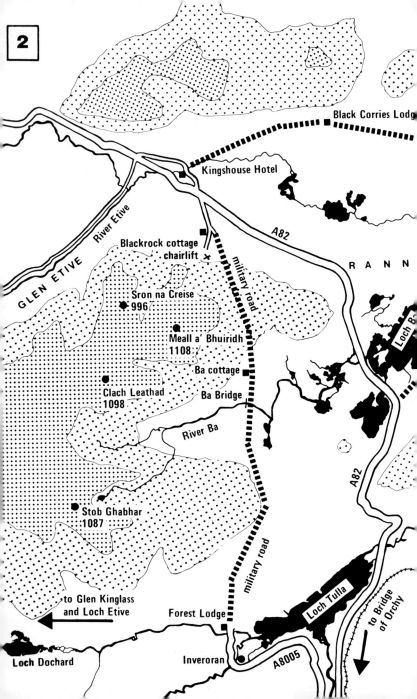

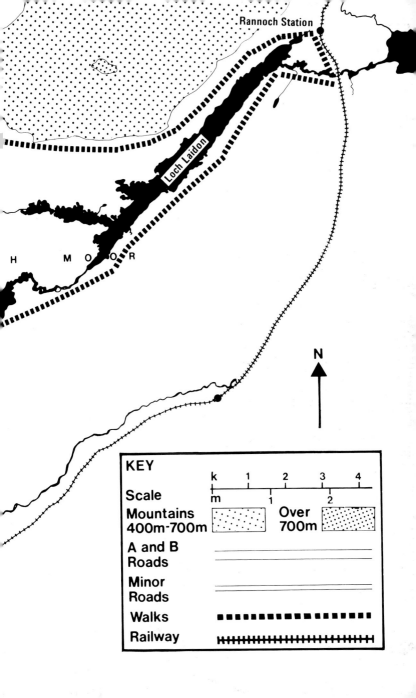

Tulla to Kingshouse road-end. There is evidence of forest burning on the Moor from early times. It was a policy of the Vikings and there are also records of the woods of Rannoch and Lochaber being destroyed to rid the area of wolves. According to tradition, there were local guides to lead travellers through the forest in former days.

The Moor still has a notorious reputation – for bogginess, but not all of its fifty-six square miles are wet. In fact it possesses many fine walks and the numerous peat hags and lochans can be avoided. For example, the walk from the main road, along the south shore of Loch Ba and then by the south shore of Loch Laidon can be followed to Rannoch station; this trek gives a profound feeling of isolation. For the less fit, there is a train back to Bridge of Orchy. Otherwise, the north shore of Loch Laidon can be traversed, past tiny and enticing sandy bays towards Kingshouse Hotel. This is a great area for birds: swans, black and red throated divers in the breeding season, ducks, and sometimes an eagle or peregrine can be seen hunting from its haunt on Clach Leathad or Meall a' Bhuiridh. The latter part of the journey is made easier by using the Black Corries to Kingshouse road. The distance from the station at Rannoch to Kingshouse is thirteen miles.

Kingshouse Hotel was a stance, an overnight stop, in droving days. The black cattle driven to the trysts at Crieff and Falkirk came from the north and west over the hill behind Allt a' Chailleach, and, indeed, grazing rights for part of this land are still held by the Glencoe crofters. The drove road then continued south and east by the line of the military road past Ba cottage, which was another stance. Even today the lusher green of the stance, where the cattle grazed overnight, stands out from the surrounding heath and bog vegetation.

The upper chairlift, Meall a' Bhuiridh, Glencoe. ►

Travelling westwards along the main road the massif of Meall a' Bhuirihd (3,636ft/1,108) is seen on the left. The first chairlift development in Scotland took place on this hill, now operating in summer for tourists and in winter for skiers on a weekend basis. The first chairlift terminates at the edge of a plateau where a walk across rather boggy (or frozen) ground leads to the bottom of another chairlift and various ski tows. These slopes probably offer the best skiing in Scotland in the form of a number of runs of varied difficulty. The names of the runs and the hazards reflect the sense of humour of these ardent weekend skiers: The Haggis Trap, Mugs' Alley, The Flypaper, and Happy Valley. A good view of Meall a' Bhuiridh is obtained from Kingshouse Hotel with Stob a' Ghlais Choire on its right, forming a wide rampart with the ridge of Sron na Creise slanting down to form one portal of Glen Etive.

The energetic summer visitor can climb Meall a' Bhuiridh (Peak of the Rutting), and follow the ridge south-south-west from its summit, thus gaining a further ridge running south from Stob a' Ghlais Choire to Clach Leathad (3,602ft/1,098m) – pronounced "Clachlet". From the top of Clach Leathad it is possible to slant downwards towards the old military road by following the east ridge, then crossing the mouth of Coire an Easain to the ruins of Ba cottage. On this circuit grouse, ptarmigan, and at least one eagle may be seen.

Kingshouse Hotel is one of the oldest licensed inns in Scotland. It is superbly remote, nestling by a stream at the western end of the Rannoch Moor. Now it is fully modernised, but when Dorothy Wordsworth visited, the poet's sister was not impressed:

◄ *Stob a' Ghlais Choire from Kingshouse Hotel. The ridge, Sron na Creise, is on the right. On the far left the ridge connects with Meall a' Bhuiridh and the ski tow.*

"The house looked respectable at a distance – a large square building, cased in blue slates to defend it from storms, – but when we came close to it the outside forewarned us of the poverty and misery within. Scarce a blade of grass could be seen growing upon the open ground . . .

"The first thing we saw on entering the door was two sheep hung up, as if just killed from the barren moor, their bones hardly sheathed in flesh. After we had waited a few minutes, looking about for a guide to lead us into some corner of the house, a woman, seemingly about forty years old, came to us in a great bustle, screaming in Erse, with the most horrible guinea-hen or peacock voice I ever heard, first to one person, then another. She could hardly spare time to show us up-stairs, for crowds of men were in the house – drovers, carriers, horsemen, travellers, all of whom she had to provide with supper, and she was, as she told us, the only woman there.

"Never did I see such a miserable, such a wretched place, – long rooms with ranges of beds, no other furniture except benches, or perhaps one or two crazy chairs, the floors far dirtier than an ordinary house could be if it were never washed . . .

"We sat shivering in one of the large rooms for three quarters of an hour before the woman could find time to speak to us again; she then promised a fire in another room, after two travellers, who were going a stage further, had finished their whisky, and said we should have supper as soon as possible. She had no eggs, no milk, no potatoes, no loaf-bread, or we should have preferred tea. With length of time the fire was kindled, and, after another

◄ *Meall a'Bhuiridh, right, with Clach Leathad; far left, Stob Ghabhar. The old military road to Forest Lodge skirts the lower slopes of these peaks on this side. Coireach a'Ba is the big corrie left of centre.*

hour's waiting, supper came, – a shoulder of mutton so hard that it was impossible to chew the little flesh that might be scraped off the bones, and some sorry soup made of barley and water, for it had no other taste.

"After supper, the woman, having first asked if we slept on blankets, brought in two pair of sheets, which she begged that I would air by the fire, for they would be dirtied below-stairs. I was very willing, but behold! the sheets were so wet, that it would have been at least a two-hours' job before a far better fire than could be mustered at King's House."

Buachaille Etive Mor and Glencoe: a cirque of mountains and bloodshed

FROM KINGSHOUSE HOTEL or from the main road Buachaille Etive Mor thrusts upward from the edge of the Moor. To its right is the entrance to Glencoe, on a sunny day bright and inviting, but in rain or storm, stark and forbidding. Leftward from the toes of the Buachaille is the gateway to upper Glen Etive, with Sron na Creise guarding the opposite flank. The highest point on the Buachaille is Stob Dearg – Red Pointed Peak (3,345ft/1019m). Its name derives from the reddish rhyolite of the upper slopes. In its lower reaches sediments have yielded fossil plants that grew in Lower Old Red Sandstone times. Amongst mountaineers it is probably the most popular mountain in Scotland. Its features can easily be identified from the main road where the upturned thumb of the Crowberry tower rises close to the summit, forming the last defiant obstacle to Crowberry ridge, one of the classical rock climbs of Scotland. The savage gully

◄ *Kingshouse Hotel, Glencoe, with Buachaille Etive Mor behind.*

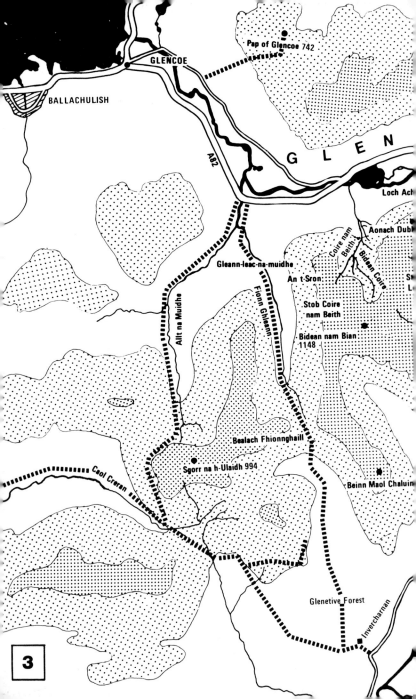

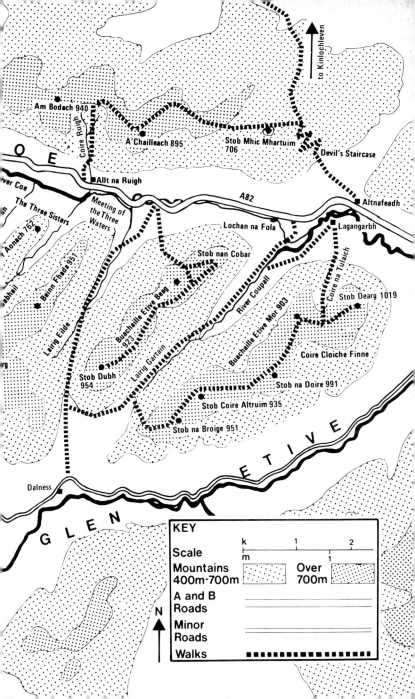

to the right of Crowberry ridge is Crowberry gully
which offers in winter a 1,000ft snow climb. Right
again is the stolid mass of the North Buttress, like a
formidable keep, presenting a bold face to the Moor.
Its right-hand side is demarked by Great Gully, an
alleyway cleaving the side of the peak, oozing with
loose scree and water in summer, and a preponder-
ance of snow in winter.

The Rannoch Moor face of the Buachaille is not for
the inexperienced. A visitor to Kingshouse in 1792,
unimpressed by its sombre countenance, wrote of,
"the carcase of the mountain, peeled sore and hide-
ously disgustful", which more than exemplifies the
axiom that beauty lies in the eye of the beholder.

The easiest means of ascent of the Buachaille,
provided there is no snow, is to take the yawning
corrie, Coire na Tulaich, immediately in front of
Altnafeadh. Cross the River Coupall at the footbridge
and skirt round the cottage of Lagangarbh. The slog
to the crest of the ridge is a monotonous one, but
once there, the walk along the open summit ridge
gives fine views, south to Ben Starav and Cruachan,
and north over the Mamores to Ben Nevis. Ballachulish Bridge can also be seen, with the rocky up-
thrust of Garbh Bheinn beyond. On a good day the
Cuillin beckon tantalisingly in the distance. From
the summit the undulating carpet of the Moor of
Rannoch is seen stretching to distant Schiehallion,
standing in shapely and isolated splendour. Care

◄ *The White Corries chairlift. Behind is Buachaille Etive
Mor and to its right the eastern entrance to Glencoe.*

The Buachaille in its winter raiment from the Glencoe road. ►

The Stob Dearg cliffs of Buachaille Etive Mor. The face ► ►
*to the right of the snow patches is the Rannoch wall,
bounded on its right by Crowberry ridge. Crowberry gully
follows the shadow line to the right of that again. Left of
the Rannoch wall with the figures on it is Curved ridge.*

should be exercised on the Buachaille in the event of mist or cloud. For descent, if visibility is bad, go 300 yards west-south-west (magnetic) on the level summit crest, then 300 yards due west to the col at the top of Coire na Tulaich. It is also possible to drop down to Glen Etive from here by going south down Coire Cloiche Finne; this latter entails a two and a half mile walk back to the main Glencoe road.

An energetic alternative on a good day is to take in all the tops of Buachaille Etive Mor: Stob Dearg, Stob na Doire (3,250ft/991m), Stob Coire Altruim (3,065ft/ 935m) and finally Stob na Broige (3,120ft/951m); then to go down the south-west nose of this peak to the valley. The face falling south-eastwards into Glen Etive should on no account be attempted, due to steep gullies and cliffs. If the descent is made to the Lairig Gartain from the summit of Stob na Broige, this valley can then be followed back to reach the Glencoe road either just east of Lochan na Fola or at Altnafeadh. The barrier of peaks on the left, to the west of the Lairig Gartain, is formed by Buachaille Etive Beag. This isolated ridge separates the two great corridors which run from Glencoe into Glen Etive, the Lairig Gartain and the Lairig Eilde, to its west. Buachaille Etive Beag (3,029ft/923m) offers one of the easiest of Glencoe hill walks and, though not outstanding as a viewpoint, nevertheless provides a worthwhile outing. Stob nan Cobar is the northerly peak, and Stob Dubh (3,129ft/954m) the southerly. Viewed from Glen Etive, Stob na Broige and Stob

---

◄ *A Brochan spectre as seen on Crowberry tower, Buachaille Etive Mor.*

Stob Dearg (Buachaille Etive Mor) as seen from close to ► *Altnafeadh. The access gully to the summit is behind the cottage of Lagangarbh.*

Looking west into Glencoe from above Altnafeadh. On the ► ► *left is the Lairig Gartain and to the right of the trees is the start of the Devil's Staircase.*

Dubh present strikingly similar profiles.

Close to the main road, half a mile west of Altnafeadh, is a small lochan nestling under the flank of Buachaille Etive Beag. Lochan na Fola means the Lochan of Blood and this tranquil pool commemorates a bloody incident in 1543 when a party of Rannoch clansmen stole cattle from Cunningham of Glenure. When the raid was discovered, Cunningham and his nine sons followed the spoor and realised their beasts were destined to cross the Rannoch Moor by way of Glencoe. So they took a short cut and surprised the raiders resting by the lochan. With their backs to the dazzling sun, the Cunninghams charged and killed several of the thieves whose bodies were then thrown into the water.

At Altnafeadh the old military road cuts northwards over the Devil's Staircase. This was built by General Caulfield, a successor to General Wade. On February 12th, 1692, eight hundred troops left Fort William and marched to the Devil's Staircase to cut off the retreat of any MacDonalds who tried to escape from the impending massacre of Glencoe. The soldiers were themselves pinned down there by a blizzard. Today, several people can still remember horse-drawn coaches being taken over the Staircase. Passengers who were fit were asked to walk this section.

The six-mile walk over to Kinlochleven is well worth doing. From the top of the pass the great barrier of hills to the north is seen to advantage with the Mamores providing an elegant foreground to the more prodigious peaks of the Aonachs and Ben Nevis; the Ben dominating all with its Moby Dick obesity. To the right lies Blackwater Dam, the western end of the Blackwater Reservoir. The construction of this reservoir prompted Patrick McGill who worked as a navvy on the project to write his novel *Children of the Dead End*. Even in the depths of

◀ *Buachaille Etive Beag from the "Bloody Lochan".*

winter the labourers braved the heights of the Staircase to reach the pub at Kingshouse. There are subsequent tales of skeletons being found in the spring snows, clutching empty whisky bottles!

The first few peaks of the Aonach Eagach can be traversed westwards, starting from the summit of the Staircase. This takes one from Stob Mhic Mhartuim to A'Chailleach (2,938ft/895m), keeping the precipitous cliffs on the right. From A'Chailleach drop down into Coire Ruigh, to the cottage of Allt na Ruigh. The further traverse of the remaining section of the ridge from the peak of Am Bodach to the Pap of Glencoe is not recommended except to experienced hill walkers, and not at all in winter except to those with winter climbing experience.

Glencoe has had many distinguished visitors. In 1841 Dickens was not too complimentary about what he saw. "The pass is an awful place. There are scores of glens high up, which form such haunts as you might imagine yourself wandering in the very height and madness of a fever . . ." Beyond Lochan na Fola the old road diverges rightwards and leads down past the Study, an unfortunate corruption of stiddie, or anvil, which is situated above the gorge of Glencoe. The old Gaelic name for this rock is Innean a' Cheathaich, the Anvil of the Mist. It can also be reached from the lay-by just beyond the gorge water-

◄ *Looking up to the Lairig Gartain (the pass in the centre of the photograph) from Glen Etive. The peak to the right is Stob na Broige and that on the left, Stob Dubh.*

The Aonach Eagach ridge, Glencoe. ►

Looking up Glencoe from the west. The Aonach Eagach ► ►
ridge is on the left and Aonach Dubh on the right. The National Trust Information Office is in the shadow, to the left of the main road.

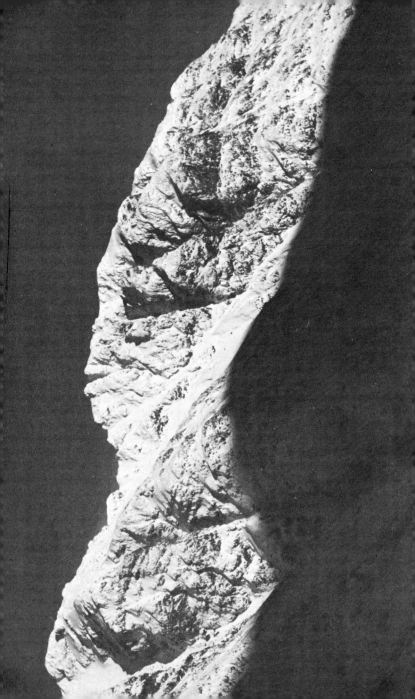

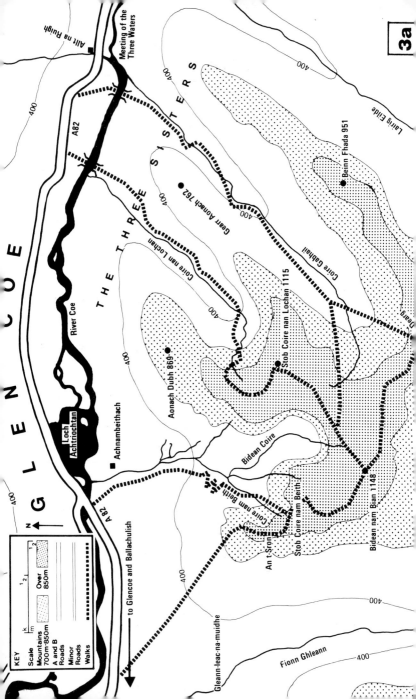

fall; a short way up the hill one gains the old road and, above, the flat topped rock of the Anvil is seen. Queen Victoria enjoyed a picnic here in 1873, but Macauley's famous painting of the same spot depicts a scene of gloom and desolation.

The Three Sisters of Glencoe rise on the left, two inclining to stoutness, but the middle sister – Gearr Aonach (2,500ft/762m) – appears slim and elegant. Her sisters, Beinn Fhada (3,120ft/951m) and Aonach Dubh (2849ft/869m), share with Gearr Aonach two valleys running into the heart of the Bidean massif. The first, Coire Gabhail, or the Lost Valley, is the famous natural pen which the MacDonalds used for hiding stolen cattle. A great landslide from the east of Gearr Aonach successfully blocked the entrance to this glen and thus formed a flat area, the size of several football pitches, which can be reached by a bridge close to the Meeting of the Three Waters.

The ridge of Beinn Fhada is seen to curve round the head of the Lost Valley; then rises to the peak of Bidean nam Bian (3,766ft/1,148m), the highest peak in Argyll. The steep flanks of Gearr Aonach which bound the Lost Valley on the right, as you look into it, merge higher up with the summit ridge of Stob Coire nan Lochan. Stob Coire nan Lochan in turn connects with Bidean via a short narrow ridge with an appropriate *bealach*, or saddle. This separates the upper basins of the Lost Valley from the Bidean Coire on the other side. A further ridge runs from the top of Bidean west-north-west over a subsidiary peak to Stob Coire nam Beith. From beyond this peak a descent can be made from the low point on the ridge into Coire nam Beith, provided there is no hard snow. However,

The Three Sisters, Glencoe. On the left is the Lost Valley ▶
with the Bealach Dearg at its head. Gearr Aonach is the
centre peak with Aonach Dubh on the right.

Gearr Aonach and Aonach Dubh in springtime. ▶ ▶

this ridge continues in a horseshoe to terminate on An t-Sron. The best route to the top (or down) from this last named peak takes the long, easy nose or *sròn*, to the main road just west of the National Trust Information Centre.

There are many combinations of hill walks to be made in the Glencoe complex. From Coire Gabhail, the Beinn Fhada-Bidean ridge is best gained by ascending to the Bealach Dearg, the pass at the head of the valley. An alternative route to the tops is to ascend the Coire nan Lochan burn by first crossing the bridge over the River Coe, a short way above Achtriochtan farm, and then climbing to gain the path. It is best to keep fairly high at the entrance to the valley; the track then follows the true right of the Coire nan Lochan burn. Once the corrie is reached, you should continue right again to gain the easy angled ridge which leads up over the main cliffs of Stob Coire nan Lochan from right to left. To the right, as you approach the start of this ridge, is Aonach Dubh, seen from this angle as a wide rocky

---

◄ *A gathering in Glencoe. To the left of the sheep is a path which leads down to the bridge over the River Coe and gives access to the Lost Valley path.*

Coire Gabhail, the Lost Valley, where the MacDonalds ►
reputedly hid stolen cattle. The path continues beyond the flat area and follows the true left of the stream to the head of the valley. Bealach Dearg is the low point on the ridge to left of centre and this gives access to the ridge leading up to Bidean, out of sight on the right.

The upper region of the Lost Valley, Glencoe, in winter. ► ►
On the left skyline is the Bealach Dearg pass. To its right, with its head in the clouds, is Bidean nam Bian. To the right of Bidean is the col leading on to Stob Coire nan Lochan. From this col, and also from Bealach Dearg, routes go to the gorge, in the lower centre of picture, to join the main path, which follows the true left of the gorge.

summit. Ahead from the crest, the backdrop of lower Glencoe is revealed, making the long slog up the Coire nan Lochan valley seem worthwhile. Beyond are Loch Leven and the foothills of the Mamores.

There is no easy way for the inexperienced down the face below. However, to continue to the top of Stob Coire nan Lochan presents no difficulty and, as already indicated, it is also possible to continue to the summit of Bidean nam Bian and return to the road either via the Bealach Dearg, or Coire nam Beith or from An t-Sron. The descent into the Bidean Coire from the *bealach* between Stob Coire nan Lochan and Bidean is not advised, but it is easy enough to drop down into the upper basin of Coire Gabhail, provided you bear left lower down, thereby avoiding a gorge. The path up Coire Gabhail, in the upper reaches, takes the true left of the stream, at a higher level.

To reach Coire nam Beith, or the Bidean Coire, you should leave the road at Loch Achtriochtan; there is a car park in the quarry at the road junction. The route follows the true left of the stream leading into the defile between An t-Sron and the west face of Aonach

---

◄ *Stob Coire nan Lochan from the summit ridge of Gearr Aonach. The recommended route to the summit of Stob Coire nan Lochan follows the valley on the right from the main road, ascends the slope between the second and third figures to reach the corrie. From there a traverse right takes one on to the right skyline ridge, which is held to the summit.*

Aonach Dubh, with the snowy top of Stob Coire nan Lochan above and to the right the twin buttresses of Bidean nam Bian. Right of that is Stob Coire nam Beith. The peak in shadow on the right is An t-Sron. The path into the Bidean Coire starts from the main road bridge, left, then heads up to the true left of the waterfall. ►

The ridge running west from the summit of Bidean nam Bian, Glencoe. ► ►

Dubh on the left, past the waterfall. This is sometimes referred to as Ossian's Shower Bath. The ascent of Bidean can be made following the right branch of the stream higher up at the junction of the corries and thus gaining the low part of the ridge between An t-Sron and Stob Coire nam Beith. The left fork of the stream leads into the Bidean Coire and from its floor the twin buttresses of Bidean stand out in stark grandeur. The one to the left is the Diamond Buttress, and to the right is the Churchdoor. If you look closely, to the right of the gully which divides them, the arch of the Churchdoor can be discerned. The squat pinnacle moored amidships in the gully is known as Collie's Pinnacle, named after the late Professor Norman Collie, a pioneer climber. Though it is possible to gain the top of Bidean by going either right of Churchdoor Buttress, or left of Diamond, these routes are not recommended, due to loose scree. Besides, snow lies on these northerly slopes well into the summer and may be hard and therefore dangerous.

Other hill walks within the general area of the glen include the Pap of Glencoe which, despite its inferior altitude, offers one of the best views in the district; the ascent is made from the old road close to Glencoe village. There are also a wide variety of low-level walks, especially at the westerly end of the glen. Full details of these can be obtained from the National Trust Information Centre, just off the main road across the River Coe from Clachaig Inn.

The Fionn Ghleann cuts upwards between Beinn Maol Chaluim and Sgorr na h-Ulaidh by the Bealach Fhionnghaill at 1,000ft, before dropping down into the new forest of Glen Etive. Another low level route leads up Gleann-leac-na-muidhe and follows the Allt

◀ *Carrying a coffin to the boat for burial on Eilean Munde. Glencoe village and the Pap of Glencoe in the background.*

na Muidhe up its steep-sided valley with the wide north face of Sgorr na h-Ulaidh (3,258ft/994m) ahead. By bearing right a high, but easy pass takes you into the head of Glen Creran where a forestry road is encountered some way down. An alternative is to follow the Caol Creran up to the watershed and descend to Glen Etive where, again, good forest roads make progress that bit easier.

On a grassy hillside, above the fanks, just beyond the Gleann-leac-na-muidhe farm, is the ruin of the summer sheiling of MacIain, the Chief of the Mac-Donald clan. It has been suggested that this was the spot where he was murdered during the notorious massacre of Glencoe, but this seems unlikely, for there was a heavy snow cover on that fateful day in 1692 and he was more likely to have been living in the comfort, albeit temporary, of his own home at Invercoe.

The lands of Glencoe were originally owned as part of the Lordship of Lorn by the MacDougalls, but they eventually lost them because of their opposition to King Robert the Bruce. He granted the lands to Angus Og of Islay, the father of the First Lord of the Isles. They then descended to his bastard son, Iain Og nan Fraoch, Young John of the Heather. The Glencoe MacDonalds were descended from Young John of the Heather, from whom they acquired their family crest, a heather bush, and also the patronymic form of their name: MacIain. At the forfeiture of the lands and titles of the Lord of the Isles by James IV the twenty merk land of Glencoe passed to the Stewarts of Appin, who were then the feudal superiors of the MacDonald chiefs.

In 1689 the Glencoe men, together with other

◄ *Looking over Glencoe village to the west face of Aonach Dubh, with Stob Coire nan Lochan behind. The ridge of An t-Sron, right, is seen leading up over Stob Coire nam Beith and on to Bidean.*

clans, fought at Killiecrankie for the Stewart King, James II of England and VII of Scotland, who had lost his throne to William of Orange that same year. Though they won the battle, the clans lost their leader with Viscount Dundee's death, but they still remained loyal to King James. Since it was against the policy of Glencoe men, like most Highlanders of that time, to come home empty-handed, they joined up with the MacDonalds of Keppoch, and raided the lands of Glenlyon, taking off several hundred cattle, horses and sheep, as well as plunder from the houses.

At this time, William III was fully committed to a war with France, and keen to subdue the rebel Scots in case the threatened French invasion materialised. The Earl of Breadalbane, who is described as being "Cunning as a fox; wise as a serpent, but slippery as an eel", tried, unsuccessfully, to buy the allegiance of the Chiefs for King William at a meeting at Achallader near Bridge of Orchy, in June 1691. He then accused Glencoe of stealing some of his cows, and MacIain, upon returning home to Glencoe, told his sons that the Earl was intent on revenge.

After the abortive meeting at Achallader, the King proclaimed a pardon for the rebels if they took an oath of allegiance before January 1st, 1692. MacIain of Glencoe and the other chiefs sent to their King – James, at St. Germain, for his consent. Few submissions were received before December and John Dalrymple, Master of Stair, who was the Secretary of State, admitted to Breadalbane in a letter that he was considering alternative plans for "mauling" the malingerers, (the mauling had been advocated by the Earl himself some time before).

The reason for the delay on the part of the chiefs was, of course, the hope of a French landing in Scotland, but when there was no sign of it occurring, all the mainland chiefs – with the exception of Glengarry and MacIain – made their submission. Royal permission for MacIain to take the oath of allegiance did not arrive until December 31, 1691, when he set off immediately for Fort William and presented himself to Colonel Hill, the Governor of the Fort. However, as the oath could only be administered by a civil magistrate, the Colonel "would not even let him stay for a drink", but sent MacIain straight off to Inveraray with a letter to Campbell of Ardkinglas, the Sheriff Depute, hoping that he could accept submission from "this great lost sheep, Glencoe".

MacIain was an old man. He could not take the usual short cut through the glens due to the severe weather, and his journey was hampered by a snow storm and by Government troops at Barcaldine. Upon arrival at Inveraray on January 2nd, he found that Ardkinglas was away. The Sheriff-Depute did not return until the 5th and was reluctant to administer the oath at that late date. Finally he did so on the 6th, with the warning that the case would have to be submitted to the Privy Council in Edinburgh. Ardkinglas also advised Colonel Hill of what had taken place and asked the Governor to take the clan under his protection. MacIain returned home under the impression that all was well.

The Clerks of the Council, however, receiving the list of those who had taken the oath, held that the inclusion of MacIain's name was invalid, since he had signed after the prescribed date. Several other members of Council, when consulted, adhered to this view; the document was accepted but MacIain's name deleted and so his case never came officially before the Privy Council.

The dirty work then began! The Master of Stair wrote from London on January 7th to inform Sir Thomas Livingstone, who was then Commander in Chief in Scotland, that troops would presently be ordered to ravage the lands of Glengarry, Locheil, Keppoch, Appin and Glencoe, adding, "I hope the soldiers will not trouble the Government with prisoners". However, by the 9th, all except Glengarry had submitted, about which he voiced his regret to Livingstone. The Master of Stair forwarded the King's instructions to Livingstone on the 11th to take action against those who had not yet taken the oath, but to offer terms first. In a covering letter the Secretary of State remarked that Argyll (an enemy of Glencoe) had told him MacIain had not submitted. "I rejoice," he wrote. "It's a great work of charity to be exact in rooting out that damnable sept, the worst in the Highlands."

Since early December Breadalbane and the Master of Stair had been planning the massacre. Dalrymple had written, "The winter is the only season in which we are sure the Highlanders cannot escape us, nor carry their wives, bairns and cattle to the mountains." The Master forwarded additional King's instructions to Livingstone on January 16th, authorising the Commander in Chief to offer terms to Glengarry, despite the fact that he had not submitted on the prescribed date, but concluded, "If M'Kean of Glencoe and that tribe can be well separated from the rest, it will be a proper vindication of the public justice to extirpate that sept of thieves . . . I entreat that the thieving tribe in Glencoe may be rooted out in earnest."

It is perhaps worth explaining why the Glencoe men were singled out when it was almost an honourable occupation for a Highlander to reive cattle, and similar unflattering comments could have been levelled against any of the clans at that time. Unfortunately, the MacDonalds of Glencoe bordered with powerful neighbours to whom they were a constant nuisance and, furthermore, their booty was always well hidden in places like Coire Gabhail and therefore difficult to recover. Obviously this was a heaven-sent opportunity to eradicate the MacDonalds, or so the Campbells and Breadalbane must have thought, and there seems little doubt that the influence of these two hereditary foes added spite to the pen of the Secretary of State.

It was on February 1st, 1692 that a company of 120 men of Argyll's regiment arrived in Glencoe, under the command of Captain Robert Campbell of Glenlyon. He told the chief's eldest son, John, that the garrison in Fort William was overcrowded and that they were to be quartered on the people of the glen. He gave his word that they had no ill intentions. This caused no suspicion at the time, as soldiers from both Argyll's and Hill's regiments were also, on the Governor's orders, billeted in the neighbourhood. Glencoe was at this time a scattered community with no less than ten small villages between Achtriochtan and Loch Leven; the land was extensively cultivated. The captain took up his quarters at Inverrigan which was a hamlet between the present Forestry Commission camp site and the village, close to where the Carnoch restaurant now stands.

As was customary in the Highlands, the troops were well entertained for a fortnight or so. Captain Campbell, who was related to the wife of Alexander, MacIain's youngest son, used to visit their house every day and drink with them; on February 12th, he played cards with both of the chief's sons. But as he sat with them, he already had his instructions for the day to come:

> You are hereby ordered to fall upon the Rebells, the McDonalds of Glenco, and putt all to the sword under seventy, you are to have speciall care that the old fox and his sones do upon no account escape your hands, you are to secure all the avenues that no man escape. This you are to putt in execution at fyve of the clock precisely . . .
>
> Ro. Duncanson.

During the night John MacDonald was aroused by soldiers calling at his window. He was at a loss to know what this could mean and went to Inverrigan where he found Captain Campbell and his men up and preparing their arms. In all probability the soldiers who roused him intended to convey a warning of the impending onslaught. But he was told that the preparations were for an action against a party of Glengarry's men, so he returned to his house and went back to bed.

During the early hours of the morning a blizzard raged and in the darkness, at five a.m., the soldiers fell about their hosts. John was wakened this time by a servant who told him that a party of twenty soldiers was approaching with fixed bayonets. Both he and his brother took to the hills from where they could hear shots in various parts of the glen.

It is not known whether the old chief was living in his house at Invercoe, or at his sheiling in Gleann-leac-na-muidhe. The latter seems unlikely since it was most probably used as a summer base and unfrequented in the winter. However, the details of his slaughter are not lacking. Lieutenant Lindsay arrived with a party of soldiers and, shouting in a friendly manner, they were allowed inside, whereupon they shot the chief in the back as he was getting out of bed. Then they stripped his wife of all her clothing and

---

◄ *It is possible that MacIain was murdered here at his summer sheiling above Gleann-leac-na-muidhe, Glencoe, though it is more likely that he was killed at his home in Invercoe.*

The Celtic Cross in a Carnoch side road close by the ►
river, "In memory of MacIain, Chief of Glencoe, who fell with his people in the massacre of Glencoe." The chief was buried on Eilean Munde, the burial isle in Loch Leven. This photograph was taken on a February 13th.

Highlanders in Glencoe. ► ►

pulled the rings from her fingers with their teeth; she was so brutally beaten up that she died. Two other men in the house were killed and another badly wounded.

Throughout the glen the slaughter was indiscriminate; old men and babies were similarly despatched. Some were burned alive in their houses when the thatch was set alight. Glenlyon's soldiers at Inverrigan tied up nine men and shot them, including their host.

At Achnacon Sergeant Barber and the soldiers billeted there fired a volley into a group of nine men sitting round a fire, killing five; the others pretended to be dead. Achtriochtan was in the group; a servant called Kennedy threw himself in front of his master and thereby shared his fate. Sergeant Barber then asked Achnacon if he was still alive. "I live," was the answer, "and I have but one wish – if I must die, to die out of doors."

"I have eaten your bread," Barber replied, "so I will do you that kindness." Achnacon was taken outside but before they could shoot he threw his plaid over the muzzles of the rifles and, escaping through the cordon, took to the mountains. The four others inside who shammed death also escaped out of the back window. The sergeant soon finished off the rest at Achnacon and the bodies of the dead were flung on the midden. One child was never seen again – only a small hand was found.

No doubt, some of the soldiers must have been sympathetic to the MacDonalds, despite the carnage. Of the 150 souls in the Glen, only forty were actually killed, though many more succumbed to the blizzard when they took to the hills. A story was told by one of the soldiers many years later, whilst accepting the hospitality of a MacDonald. He told how, when ordered by his officer to kill a child, he cut off only a

A view of Garbh Bheinn in Ardgour, from Glencoe.

little finger, sparing the infant and returning to his superior with the "evidence". His host listened silently to the tale and then held up a hand with a missing little finger.

The MacDonalds who survived the massacre put in a claim to the Government for the livestock driven away by the troops: between 1,400 and 1,500 cows, 500 horses, as well as many sheep and goats. The total number appears to be on the high side, but it was no doubt subject to bargaining . . . They resettled the glen and, during 1715 and 1745, fought again for the Stewarts.

Parliament denounced the massacre as "Murder under Trust", the definition in Scots law of a crime so terrible that it carried quadruple penalties: hanging, disembowelling, beheading and quartering. In those times hospitality was an almost sacred concept and it was its breach which so stirred public opinion against the deed. As long as people continue to travel through the dark and sometimes snowy portals of Glencoe, the massacre will be talked about and the name of Campbell be synonymous with treachery.

Ballachulish to Castle Stalker

BEINN A' BHEITHIR, Peak of the Thunderbolt, dominates the old slate village of Ballachulish. The traverse of the summits of this massif provides a satisfying and view-filled day. There are five main tops, but the horseshoe ridge to Sgorr Dhearg (3,362ft/ 1,025m), then on to Sgorr Dhonuill (3,284ft/1,001m) usually satisfies all but the most ardent peak baggers.

Access to the hill path is gained by a forest road, the entrance to which is a short distance west of St. John's Church on the A828. Do not follow the right-hand bend in the forest road, but instead go directly

uphill beside the stream to join the hill path. This track winds its way from the forest up to the nose of Beinn Bhan which overlooks Ballachulish. An alternative ascent can be made from Gorteneorn farm. Beyond here the top of Sgorr Bhan is reached after treadmilling a scree path. The elegant symmetry of the horseshoe ridge now leads the eye (and the feet) to Sgorr Dhearg. Down, then up again, and Sgorr Dhonuill is reached, followed by a gentle descent to the col beyond, where a way down the corrie to the Gleann a' Chaolais forest is obvious. Turning either left or right at the forestry road makes a pleasant finale to the walk which ends on the main road close to Ballachulish Ferry Hotel.

It is worth bearing in mind that these forest roads are excellent for bad weather walking. To the south and west, down the coast, Duror and Salachan glens offer equally fine evergreen alleyways. Further, longer, walks can be enjoyed from West Laroch, Ballachulish. One takes the true left bank of the River Laroch from Gorteneorn farm to the forest road in Glen Duror; a short section of this route is pathless, but the direction is obvious. Provided transport is arranged at the far end, it offers a fine few hours through wild country. Alternatively, the path from West Laroch can be followed to its true destination, Glen Creran. At one time this track was an old clan route. Care should be taken after fording the River Laroch just beyond a cairn, since the path on the ascent to the ridge and the stile over the forest fence is not immediately clearly defined.

Castle Stalker (rightly Stalcair, meaning Hunter) guards the entrance of Loch Laich in Appin, as it has

---

◄ *Looking across Loch Leven to Beinn a'Bheithir on the right.*

Beinn a'Bheithir, above Ballachulish. ►

The horseshoe ridge, Beinn a'Bheithir. ► ►

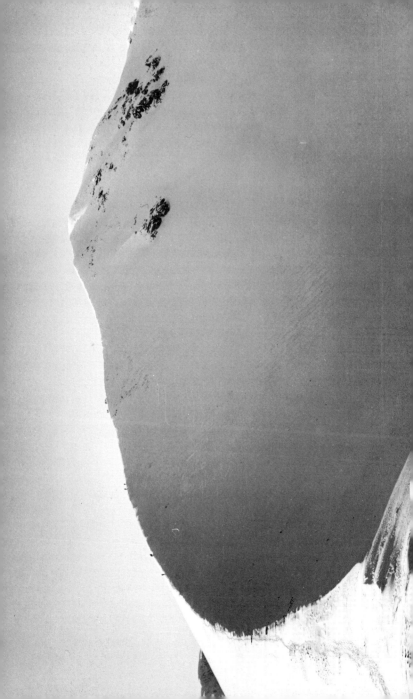

done since the thirteenth century. Traditionally, the castle passed from the MacDougalls to the Stewarts in 1388, together with the Lordship of Lorn. It was also supposed to have been restored around the 1490s and James IV used it during his tours of the Western Isles. It was rebuilt in its present form in the first half of the sixteenth century.

The walls are nine feet thick and there are four storeys, capped by a flush parapet, a wall-walk and an attic with a gabled caphouse at the stairhead. The gateway leads by a stairway to the first floor which is guarded from above by a parapet, suitably furnished with holes for pouring boiling oil and lead on the heads of unwelcome visitors. The first floor hall has a fireplace and stone seats. There is also a pit, or prison, hewn from the base rock to accommodate those currently out of favour.

In 1463 the third Stewart Lord of Lorn was murdered at Dunstaffnage Castle in a revolt organised by the MacDougalls and Campbells. However his son, Dugald, with the support of the people of Lorn and the MacLarens of Perthshire held on to Appin and Castle Stalker and he defeated the MacDougalls at the Battle of Stalc in 1468, which was fought at nearby Portnacroish. Alan MacDougall, his father's murderer, was killed in the conflict, besides several hundred others. In the graveyard of the Episcopal Church at Portnacroish a granite slab carries an inscription commemorating the battle.

Ballachulish Bridge is not man's most elegant edifice, neither is the rather cumbersome memorial to James of the Glen which adorns the southerly portals

◄ *The peaks of the Mamores on the far left and the Pap of Glencoe, right of centre, from Beinn a'Bheithir. The village of Ballachulish is to the left, in shadow.*
The old ferry at the Ballachulish narrows. Behind are the ►
peaks of Glencoe with Bidean right of centre.
Castle Stalker, Appin. ► ►

on their western side. It was at this spot that James Stewart of Acharn was executed in 1752 "for a crime of which he was not guilty". It all started after the 'Forty-five, when the lands of the Stewarts were forfeited (including Castle Stalker). One of the hated Campbells, Colin Campbell of Glenure, who was known as the Red Fox was appointed the Government Factor in Appin. He evicted Stewarts and replaced them with members of his clan. The Red Fox was shot whilst passing through Kentallen in the company of several mounted men, on his way to implement more evictions. His murderer escaped unseen. James was accused of the crime, though many had better motives than he, and he stood a farcical trial at Inveraray before the Lord Justice General of Scotland (the Duke of Argyll) and a jury of eleven chosen Campbells! Despite lack of any evidence, James was hanged at sunset. They then secured the body by chains to the gallows and there it hung for two months, under guard until it disintegrated. The skeleton was then wired and re-hung. James's much displayed bones were eventually laid to rest one dark night – by a son of the forfeited Ardsheal – in the small graveyard on the south side of Cuil Bay at Keil.

Kinlochleven to Fort William by the military road; and by Loch Eilde Mor to Glen Nevis

KINLOCHLEVEN MIGHT BE described as a deplorable town in a delectable setting. Despite its unattractive appearance, the town, which owes its very being to the British Aluminium Company, provides much needed employment in a depressed region. Yet five minutes from the main street, and you are afoot in the wild hills of the Mamores. Here old roads steal

A telephoto shot of Loch Leven with Kinlochleven at the head. ▶

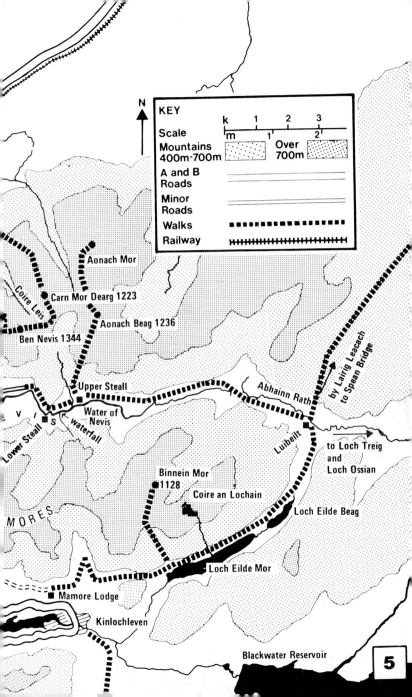

KEY

Scale

Mountains
400m-700m — Over 700m

A and B Roads

Minor Roads

Walks ████████

Railway ++++++++

Aonach Mor

Carn Mor Dearg 1223

Aonach Beag 1236

Ben Nevis 1344

Coire Leis

Upper Steall

Abhainn Rath

by Lairig Leacach to Spean Bridge

Water of Nevis waterfall

Lower Steall

N E V I S

Luibeilt

to Loch Treig and Loch Ossian

Binnein Mor 1128

Coire an Lochain

Loch Eilde Beag

M O R E S

Loch Eilde Mor

Mamore Lodge

Kinlochleven

Blackwater Reservoir

5

between the heights to Glen Nevis, and north and east to Spean Bridge and Loch Treig, offering fabulous walking through unspoiled country: the home of the red deer, the fox, and the blue hare. Six hundred feet above Kinlochleven, perched on the toes of the Mamores, is Mamore Lodge. This imposing West Highland house was used as a shooting lodge by King Edward VII. It is situated close to the old military road which leads to Fort William and is a continuation of the road over the Devil's Staircase. It is worthwhile to walk the fifteen miles into Fort William, though the last five miles are surfaced road. If the full distance is too far, then a descent to Callert on Loch Leven can be made from Lairigmor, or to Onich from a point two and a half miles further on at Lochan Lunn Da-Bhra (there is no path for about one mile), descending into Gleann Righ.

Kinlochleven to Glen Nevis also makes a fine day's outing. The footpath leading out of the town on the north side takes one up the hillside to Loch Eilde Mor, to join the main track from Mamore Lodge to Luibeilt. At this point a small path continues uphill and an ascent of Binnein Mor (3,700ft/1,128m) can be made, via Coire an Lochain; this is one of the finest viewpoints in the Mamores. The Luibeilt track continues on the north-west side of Loch Eilde Mor; then skirts its little sister, Loch Eilde Beag. At Luibeilt, turn west for the Glen Nevis track. A further trail continues, however, northwards to connect up with the Lairig Leacach, where the old "Road to the Isles" – in the form of a respectable track –

◄ *Loch Leven with the Pap of Glencoe and Mamore Lodge near centre. The track leading into the Mamores is to the right of the Lodge.*

Ben Nevis from upper Glen Nevis, Steall cottage in foreground. Carn Mor Dearg ridge runs down right from the summit. ►

Upper Glen Nevis and the Steall waterfall. ► ►

continues to Spean Bridge via Corriechoille, the home of the famous Lochaber Drover. But to return to the Glen Nevis branch of the path at Luibeilt, it follows the true right of the Abhainn Rath to the watershed; just over the divide one finds the Water of Nevis for company. The path takes the true right of the Nevis, past the ruins of Upper Steall, to drop down onto the tranquil floor of the valley, dominated by the Steall waterfall. Crouching in the lee of the falls is Lower Steall, now a climbers' hut. The track continues down through the Gorge of Nevis, a well-defined path on one of the most scenic routes in all Scotland, to reach the car park at the end of the Glen Nevis road.

These are only a few of the walks one can enjoy in the Mamores. A glance at the OS map will reveal many others, equally fine.

Fort William and Inverlochy Castle

FORT WILLIAM IS a hybrid of modern ticky-tacky houses and traditional building, of industry and tourism. The West Highland Museum in Cameron Square is well worth a visit, with numerous items of interest, including the Secret Portrait of Prince Charles Edward Stuart. The original fort at Fort William was built by General Monck in 1654, but it no longer exists. Inverlochy Castle still stands, however. It is reached from the main road on the north-east side of town, opposite the main entrance to the aluminium works. The original castle is reputed to have been built by the Comyn family in 1260, though it was probably sited on a still older fort. The existing castle was built around the late fifteenth century.

In 1645 the famous Battle of Inverlochy was fought on the flat ground to the south-west of the castle, between Montrose's Royalist army and the Covenant-

Inverlochy Castle with Ben Nevis behind. ▶

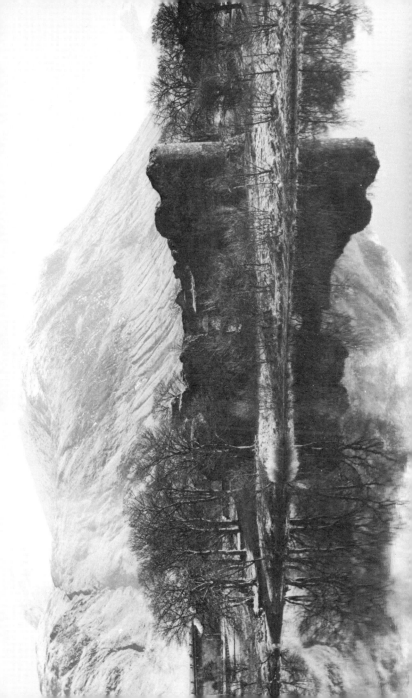

ing army under Campbell of Argyll. Montrose's march, prior to the battle, was the most strenuous and daring in Scottish military history. He was encamped close to the present Fort Augustus, which had not then been established, when news of the Covenanting army's arrival at Inverlochy was brought to him by the poet Iain Lom. Though he knew that the forces under Campbell outnumbered his by two to one, he set off on January 31st, using a devious route to reach Inverlochy, going close to the Corrieyairack Pass and eventually through Glen Spean. This took him through some of the roughest terrain in the country. By avoiding the Great Glen, where his movements would have been reported to Inverlochy, he achieved complete secrecy, and the appearance of his men outside the walls of Inverlochy on February 2nd caused trepidation amongst the ranks of the Covenanting army. Argyll was so shaken by this sudden display of resolution that he turned tail and abandoned his men, taking to his birlinn and leaving half his army to be butchered.

The Battle of Inverlochy must have been brutal; the Campbells were a hated race, as this translation of the Gaelic poem by Iain Lom, "The Day of Inverlochy", shows.

. . . I ascended early on the Sunday morning to the top of the castle of Inverlochy. I saw the whole affair, and the battle's triumph was with Clan Donald . . .

A tale most joyful to receive of the Campbells of the wry mouths – every troop of them as they came having their heads broken under the blows of the swords . . .

John of Moidart of the bright sails that would sail the ocean on a dark day, there was no tryst-breaking with you! and joyful to me was the news of Barbreck in your power . . .

Alasdair of the sharp biting blades, you promised yesterday to destroy them. You put the rout past the castle, guiding right well the pursuit.

Alasdair of the sharp galling blades, if you had had Mull's heroes with you, you had made those who escaped of them wait, while the rabble of the dulse retreated.

Alasdair, noble son of Colla, right hand for cleaving the castles, you put rout on the grey Saxons and if they drank kail-broth you emptied it out of them.

Did you know the Goirtein Odhar? Well was it manured, not with dung of sheep or goats, but with blood of Campbells frozen!

Curse you if I pity your condition, listening to the distress of your children, wailing for the band that was in the battlefield, the howling of the women of Argyle!

(from *The Golden Treasury of Scottish Verse*)

It is claimed that about 300 Camerons fought for Montrose at Inverlochy and that their piper played the pibroch, "Come sons of dogs, and I will give you flesh".

I have already mentioned Glen Nevis as the termination of the Kinlochleven walk, but it is of course much more easily accessible from Fort William, where the narrow tarmac road leaves the A82 to climb this scenic glen, with its elegant Caledonian pines.

From the top car park the walk up the gorge is a must, and within the scope of anyone. Aonach Beag (4,060ft/1,236m) can be climbed without too much difficulty. Approach it from the south, from directly above the ruins of Upper Steall. Aonach Mor can then be taken in as well, provided conditions and weather permit. From its summit there is an alternative way down to the north to the forestry roads in the Leanachan Forest.

Should you wish to remain at a lower level, take the path to Luibeilt and follow on past the cottage to reach Loch Treig or Loch Ossian (fifteen and a half miles). In summer one can stay overnight at the idyllically remote Youth Hostel at the west end of Loch Ossian.

Ben Nevis

BEN NEVIS IS the Big Brother of Lochaber – indeed, of Britain, for (at 4,408ft/1,344m) it is the country's highest mountain. From Fort William it lurks, hiding its obesity behind Meall an t-Suidhe, and it is up the southerly flank of this last-named peak that the path leaves ground level at Achintee. An alternative path crosses the River Nevis at a footbridge opposite the Glen Nevis Youth Hostel and goes directly uphill to join the Achintee track. The path to the summit of Ben Nevis is, when clear of snow, well defined.

From the halfway point at Lochan Meall an t-Suidhe, a small cairn indicates a lesser path running off leftwards (north) above the lochan. This offers an alternative route up the Ben, sneaking under the dark cliffs of the north-east face. But first, let us continue with the tourist route which rises steeply in a series of zig-zags alongside the Red Burn. Though the route from here to the summit looks as innocuous as a pavement in Princes Street, it can be hazardous to stray from it in cloud or mist. As on all other hill walks, a map and compass should be taken, and spare warm and windproof clothing. Even in mid-summer, snow storms can sweep the plateau above.

◀ *The saddle between Aonach Beag and Aonach Mor.*

Climbers at the top of Number 2 Gully, Ben Nevis. ▶

The great cliffs of Ben Nevis in winter. To the left is the ▶ ▶
Carn Mor Dearg ridge.

On the summit near the edge of the cliff are the remains of the old observatory. It fulfilled its function for collecting sunspot data and was closed down in 1904. An hotel was built on the top later, but this too is now a ruin. The records kept at the observatory are of considerable interest. Ben Nevis lies in the storm track of the North Atlantic hurricanes; during the winter months, winds regularly blow at over 100 mph – sometimes as much as 150 mph. The mean annual rainfall over the nineteen years that records were kept averaged 160.79 ins, whilst the record for any one year was 240 ins, in 1898. The gully close by the observatory ruin is still called Gardyloo (*"Gardez l'eau"*). This was a warning call in the days when people used to throw slops from their windows. Gardyloo gully was used as the rubbish shoot for the observatory.

For those still with some energy left after the climb up the Ben – three hours average – it is possible to continue round the sensational tightrope ridge to Carn Mor Dearg and descend this mountain by its northern slopes. This cirque offers unique views of the Ben Nevis cliffs and is one of the most impressive mountain walks in the entire Highlands. The descent route off Carn Beag Dearg leads down to the forestry car park. This is close to the Allt a' Mhuilinn, just past the fence. Though the forest road is usually closed to vehicular traffic, it can be followed down to

---

A rock climber's paradise. The great cliffs of Carn Mor Dearg, Ben Nevis, from the Allt a'Mhuilinn path on the north-east side of Ben Nevis.

Looking from Carn Mor Dearg towards the Mamores. On the right is the Carn Mor Dearg arete.

Carn Mor Dearg arete and the north-east buttress of Ben Nevis. Coire Leis is in the foreground below the arete. When the slopes to the arete are clear of snow access can be gained to the arete at the low point for people with hill walking experience.

Torlundy, or the more direct and boggier path taken down the side of the burn to the distillery.

Another recommended route up Ben Nevis, which fully exploits the grandeur of the north-east face, is to take the path up to the halfway lochan, as already described; then, from the fork and cairn, slant round the lower slopes of Carn Mor Dearg, above Lochan Meall an t-Suidhe, following the path which leads into the Allt a' Mhuilinn. It then closely follows the burn past the climbers' hut, to run out of steam as it rises into Coire Leis at the head of the glen. En route, one is conscious of the greatest cliffs in Britain poised above, with their fascinating complexity of buttresses and gullies. These, coupled with the fierce weather, make the Ben internationally renowned as an ice climber's paradise. But in summer it is also a fine rock climbing mountain.

One must rise out of the arena of Coire Leis to reach the crest of the Carn Mor Dearg ridge, which connects this mountain with its close companion, the Ben. This is a more sporting approach to the Ben than the ascent of the Red Burn, but if there is still hard snow, it should be strictly avoided. It is better to make a prudent retreat, rather than suffer a painful defeat! From the ridge a short view-filled grind takes one up the wide shoulder on to the summit of Ben Nevis.

◄ *The climbers' hut below the north-east cliffs of Ben Nevis.*

Carn Mor Dearg ridge, in late spring, leading over to Ben ►
Nevis.

Looking across Glen Nevis to the peaks of the Mamores ► ►
from near the summit of Ben Nevis.

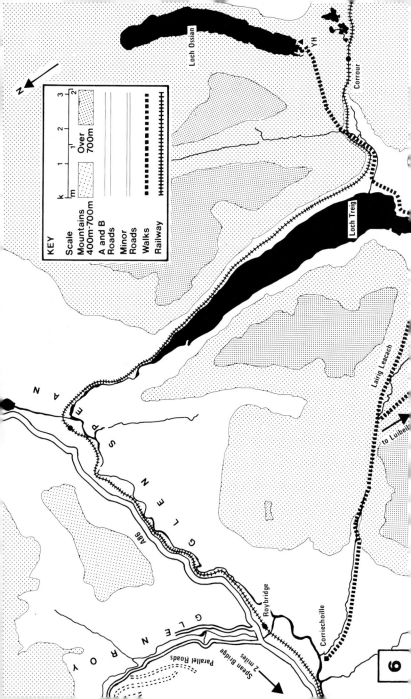

KEY

Scale

Mountains 400m–700m

Over 700m

A and B Roads

Minor Roads

Walks

Railway

Loch Ossian

YH

Corrour

Loch Treig

GLEN SPEAN

Lairig Leacach

to Luibeilt

A86

GLEN ROY

Roybridge

Corriechoille

Spean Bridge

Parallel Roads

2 miles

N

6

Glen Spean, Glen Roy
and the Road to the Isles

I MENTIONED ON pages 89–92 that a long hill route of
some eighteen and a half miles runs from Kinlochleven
to Spean Bridge via Luibeilt. From Corriechoille this
"Road to the Isles" can be retraced south on foot to
take you up the Lairig Leacach pass, then down to the
southerly end of Loch Treig. You can continue east
past this loch to cross the West Highland Line and
reach Loch Ossian and its Youth Hostel. For those
suffering from blisters after this fourteen mile walk,
the train can be taken from Corrour back to Spean
Bridge.

At Roybridge a side road runs up into the defile of
Glen Roy for a few miles. From a car park at the end
of the tarmac road the geological feature of the
Parallel Roads can be seen. These were formed at the
end of the last Ice Age when a huge glacier dammed
the outflow from the glens. The lakes this formed
developed beaches. As the water level dropped, new
beaches were successively formed at lower levels.
This part of Glen Roy is now a National Nature
Reserve.

The Youth Hostel at Loch Ossian with Ben Nevis behind. ▶

Ben Nevis, the Carn Mor Dearg arete and Aonach Beag ▶ ▶
from Loch Ossian.

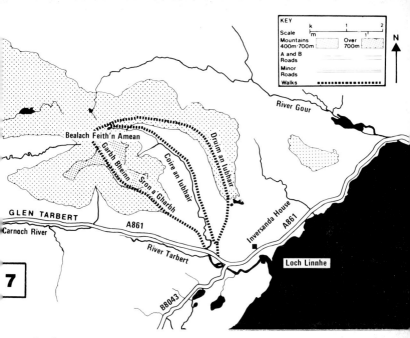

7

Ardgour:
Glen Tarbert and the Rough Mountain

THE CORRAN FERRY gives access to the lands of Morvern, Moidart and Ardnamurchan; regions of loch-indented coastline, traversed by infrequent roads, generally of the single-track variety, whose central ribbon of sump-high grass bears witness to lack of use.

This is unspoiled country: wide, open tracts of ground mainly given over to sheep and deer. For peace and quiet there is little need to head further north. This almost forgotten corner of Scotland

---

◄ *The Parallel Roads, Glen Roy.*
Corran lighthouse. ►
Garbh Bheinn from Coire an Iubhair. The ridge on the ► ►
left leads from Sron a'Gharbh, and that on the right of the
summit, to Bealach Feith 'n Amean.

contains everything, from idyllic beaches and secluded coves, to mountains, moors and rivers, with all their associated sports.

Entering Glen Tarbert, just beyond the Kingairloch turn-off, there is an old bridge on the right. Here there are several interesting alternatives for hill walking or climbing. Coire an Iubhair is the name of the rugged glen which lies between two ridges, Druim an Iubhair to the right, and Sron a' Gharbh on the left. It is a favourite haunt of the red deer. The path up the corrie tends to be boggy but the walk is rewarding for the rock walls of Garbh Bheinn rise a thousand feet on the mountain's north-east face. The main feature of Garbh Bheinn itself is the Great Ridge which leads up to the summit in a thousand-foot sweep of gneiss. It was first climbed by J. H. Bell and W. Brown in 1897.

The route up Sron a' Gharbh is more strenuous; height is gained rapidly on the rocky spur, but always keep the cliffs on the right. On the left of the Sron is Coire a' Chothruim, the source of the Carnoch River which flows into Loch Sunart at the western end of Glen Tarbert. From the summit of Garbh Bheinn (2,903ft/885m) a descent can be made to the Bealach Feith 'n Amean and down Coire an Iubhair to the road.

A less precipitous route, which affords superb views of Garbh Bheinn, is offered by the ridge to the right of Coire an Iubhair, Druim an Iubhair. It curves round the side of the glen like a giant sickle, then dips down to meet the Bealach Feith 'n Amean.

From these ridges, as also from the summit of Garbh Bheinn, there are superb views of Loch Linnhe and the westerly peaks of Argyll and Lochaber. Needless to say, neither of the ridge routes should be attempted unless the party is fit and the

◄ *The route up Sron a' Gharbh, Garbh Bheinn, from the old bridge in Glen Tarbert. Coire an Iubhair is to the right.*

weather fine, but the Coire an Iubhair path provides a less demanding alternative. During the stalking season, permission should be obtained from Inversanda House.

The A884 road follows the south side of Loch Sunart for a little while before entering the heart of Morvern, at which point a narrow branch road continues along the southern shore past Laudale House. For those who feel that the "Rough Mountain", as Garbh Bheinn is sometimes called, is best left to the wild goats, there is a pleasant walk along this track, returning the same way. The views across Loch Sunart – surely one of the finest sea lochs in Scotland – are outstanding; on the far shore the bulk of Beinn Resipol rears above Sunart, that wild tract of land between the southern end of Loch Shiel and Loch Sunart.

Into Morvern:
the rough road to Loch Teacuis and
Ardtornish's dark fortress

KINGAIRLOCH LIES ON the narrow loop road which runs south-west from the mouth of Glen Tarbert, rising over moorland before it drops down to the margin of Loch Linnhe. It then skirts under steep cliffs before reaching Kingairloch, and continues a few miles further west to rejoin the Lochaline road.

Glensanda is some five miles down the coast from Kingairloch. A track leads round Loch a' Choire and follows the shore for some way, then rises and descends again to a long-abandoned sheiling. Once again, the path climbs and soon one catches a first glimpse of Caisteal na Gruagaich (sometimes also called Nagier), set above a steeply shelving beach.

◀ *Looking across Loch Sunart to Strontian and the hills beyond from the road to Laudale House.*

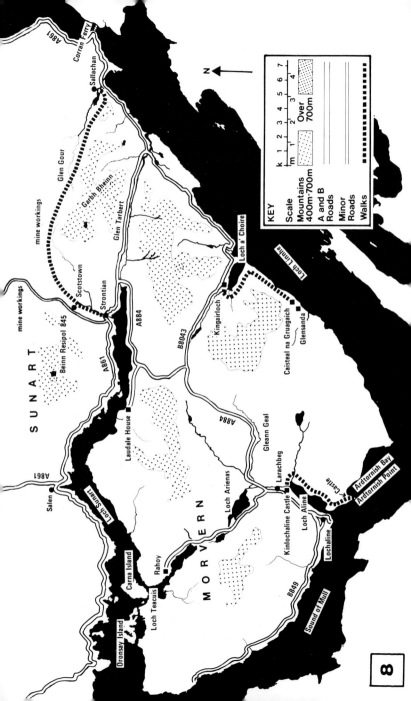

KEY

Scale

Mountains 400m–700m

Over 700m

A and B Roads

Minor Roads

Walks

N

8

SUNART

Corran Ferry

A861

Sallachan

Glen Gour

mine workings

Garbh Bheinn

Glen Tarbert

Scotstown

Strontian

Beinn Resipol 845

mine workings

A861

A884

B8043

Loch a' Choire

Loch Linnhe

Kingairloch

Caisteal na Gruagaich

Glensanda

Laudale House

A884

Gleann Geal

Loch Arienas

Larachbeg

Kinlochaline Castle

Loch Aline

Castle

Ardtornish Bay

Ardtornish Point

Lochaline

B849

Salen

A861

Loch Sunart

Carna Island

Rahoy

MORVERN

Loch Teacuis

Oronsay Island

Sound of Mull

This castle has a special fascination and not a great deal is known about its history. It was probably built in the fifteenth century as the stronghold of the Macleans of Kingairloch. It was once reputed to have been the base of a pirate called Runie who made use of it one winter whilst he plundered the neighbouring countryside. During one of his raids into Appin, across Loch Linnhe, he established camp on the hillock where Appin House now stands. A few of the natives, who were bold enough to return after the populace took fright, noted a large boulder conveniently poised above Runie's camp. Whilst the pirates were feasting, they cautiously undermined the great rock and sent it crashing through the camp below, killing the pirate chief and two of his sons. The rest of the band took to their galleys.

Close by the castle, in the still fertile lower reaches of Glensanda, stand the ruins of several houses. They bear silent witness to the depopulation which is so characteristic of the western seaboard of Scotland. Now, with the renewed interest in the crofting way of life, a future generation of children will perhaps play round the pink-grey granite walls of Caisteal na Gruagaich, and its very isolation may yet be considered a commodity of great value.

From the Lochaline road, one of the roughest roads in Scotland leads past Loch Arienas towards Loch Teacuis. The turning for these lochs is found just across the River Aline, after driving down Gleann Geal, the White Glen. It is advisable to park your vehicle and negotiate the Loch Teacuis road on foot. A mile and a half past Rahoy House is the dun of Rahoy. The path for it starts to the right of the house, behind a cottage and through a forest gate. The ruin – and it is now very much a ruin – is situated on a small hill overlooking the narrows of the loch. Before trees screened it, this dun must have had a fine outlook across the mouth of Loch Teacuis and beyond, to the

isles of Oronsay and Carna which lie in the throat of Loch Sunart. The name "Rahoy" is derived from "Rath Thuaith" – the North Fort. The dun is vitrified and during 1936-7 it was excavated by Professor V. G. Childe. Its age is uncertain but probably dates from late BC or early AD.

Further down the road to Lochaline, on the left, one passes the clachan of Larachbeg. This is the ground which was given to the people of St. Kilda when they were evacuated from their own island in 1930.

At the head of Loch Aline stands Kinlochaline Castle, a fifteenth-century tower house, reputedly the traditional home of the Clan MacInnes who were hereditary bowmen to the Clan MacKinnon. The latter clan were vassals of the Lord of the Isles. On returning from one battle, the Lord of the Isles addressed a Chief of the MacInnes: "My blessing on you, Chief of Kinlochaline. While MacDonald is in power, MacInnes shall be in favour." However, shortly afterwards, the chief had a disagreement with his overlord and, along with five of his sons, was murdered in nearby Ardtornish Castle. The MacInnes lands were then given to Maclean of Duart by a charter dated 1390. Later Kinlochaline Castle was breached and fired by Cromwell's army. It was restored in 1890. Though it is now usually locked up, a key can be obtained from the nearby cottage.

The castle is said to have been built by Lady Dhubh Chal (Black Veil) who was reputed to have paid for its construction in butter of a volume equal to that of the castle. In fact, a local name for the castle is Caisteal an Ime, "Butter Castle". The castle's walls are more than seven feet thick and above the door are openings

◀ *Caisteal na Gruagaich, Glensanda.*

Kinlochaline Castle. ▶

The ruins of Ardtornish Castle, with Mull beyond. ▶ ▶

for pouring oil and lead on besiegers. The door is now reached by a stone stairway. Above the doorway a sandstone panel contains a carving, in relief, of a stag being pursued by a hound, with a salmon below it. Inside there is a guard chamber and, on the right, a stair spirals up inside the wall to reach the main hall. A further flight of stairs continues up, then forks; one branch leads to the battlements and the other forms a level passageway before descending again into the hall – an unusual feature. Out on the battlements, which at one time only had trapdoor access, is a fireplace which the defenders used for heating up the oil and lead. On the ground floor there is a wide arched fireplace, above which is a moulded plaque of a kneeling figure – a nude female – grasping in her hand a circular object and holding a sack, or bag, against her left thigh. One can't help speculating whether there is some connection between the moulded figure and the MacInnes motto: "Pleasure is the outcome of exercise".

It is possible to continue on foot down the easterly shore of Loch Aline, past the narrows opposite Lochaline village and round the coast to Ardtornish Point where stand the ruins of Ardtornish Castle, commanding a dominating position over the Sound of Mull. It was here that Sir Walter Scott set the opening canto of his poem, "Lord of the Isles".

"Wake, Maid of Lorn!" The Minstrels sung –
Thy rugged halls, Ardtornish rung,
And the dark seas, thy towers that lave,
Heaved on the beach a softer wave . . .
Beneath the Castle's sheltering lee,
They staid their course in quiet sea,
Hewn in the rock, a passage there
Saught the dark fortress by a stair,
  So straight, so high, so steep,

With peasant's staff one valiant hand
Might well the dizzy pass have mann'd,
'Gainst hundreds arm'd with spear and brand,
   And plunged them in the deep.
His bugle then the helmsman wound;
Loud answered every echo round,
   From turret, rock and bay;
The postern hinges crash and groan,
And soon the Warder's cresset shone
On those rude steps of slippery stone,
   To light the upward way.

The castle first appears in the charters during the mid-fourteenth century, but it was probably built earlier in the century by Angus Og of Isla to whom King Robert the Bruce granted considerable territory, including Kenalbane, the early name for Morvern. Good John of Isla died in Ardtornish and his eldest son, Donald of Harlaw, as he became known, amassed his fleet for the battle of Harlaw in Ardtornish Bay. In 1462 the Treaty of Westminster and Ardtornish was signed between John, the fourth and last Lord of the Isles, and Edward IV of England, who was in need of powerful Scottish allies. The treaty gave John and his henchmen unlimited aid for the conquest of the whole of Scotland, an enterprise which was, however, unsuccessful and lost him his lands and titles. He died in the monastery of Paisley.

Today little remains of Scott's "dark fortress", but surveying the ruins of the castle one can almost feel the power which once emanated from it. The entrance was on the eastern wall. On the ground floor there is a passage which leads to a latrine tower at the north-west angle. The remains of a staircase giving access to the first floor can still be discerned beneath the turf. In the eighteenth century blocks and possibly slates were taken from the castle for the construction of Ardtornish House, now demolished, and much refacing work was necessary on the ruin in 1873. The window in the south wall dates from this period of restoration. Scott's mention of "slippery stone" remains pertinent enough, however. The castle is constructed of dressed basalt, which is extremely slippery rock when wet.

Across Ardtornish Bay, to the north-east of the castle, a sheer line of cliffs stands out from the shore. Various waterfalls, known as the Morvern Witches, overflow at intervals along this basaltic escarpment. At the highest point of the cliffs, close to a sheep fank, lies a sizeable flat stone called "the rock of the corpses". Any men condemned to death by the Chiefs of Ardtornish were hurled over the cliff from here, to crash on the rocks beneath.

Sunart and Ardnamurchan: the Bay of the Spaniards and the Great Eucrite

STRONTIAN NESTLES ON the northern shore of Loch Sunart, close to the head of the loch. It was once the centre of a thriving mining community, when lead was extracted from the old mines to the north of the town. It was here that the mineral Strontianite was first discovered in 1764.

From the narrow road leading over to Polloch there are a variety of walks. One, starting from the nature trail at Scotstown, leads eventually to more remote mine workings then bears south-east (part of the way without a path) over the watershed to Glen Gour. The true right of the River Gour should be taken, where a good track follows the last few miles to Sallachan. This provides a long trek through wild rocky country.

Close to the high point of the Polloch road is the centre of the old mining operations, which were closed in 1904. From here it is a good day's expedition to strike west and climb Beinn Resipol (2,771ft/

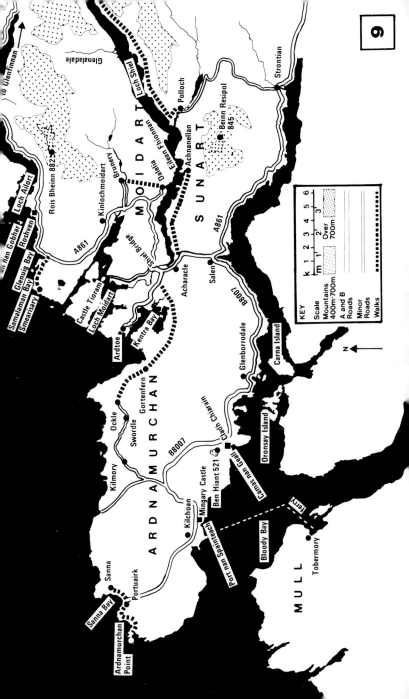

845m). It is one of the best vantage points of the whole area.

A fine variety of views is seen through the scrub oak and birch along the north shore of Loch Sunart. At Salen the road branches, the right-hand one leading over the hill across the neck of Ardnamurchan to Acharacle, whilst the other swings down round Salen Bay. A few miles beyond, the islands Carna and Oronsay are seen hugging the far shore; tucked away behind the former is Loch Teacuis. Continuing down the lochside the road is twisty and narrow, but displays a distinctive charm with its poised, moss-covered boulders and the occasional golden plover. Passing Glenborrodale, one reaches Camas nan Geall which was possibly visited by St. Columba. In a field behind this sheltered cove lies Cladh Chiarain, Ciaran's graveyard. St. Ciaran was buried here in 548. A steep track leads down to the bay which is well worth visiting.

Rising from the far side of the bay is Ben Hiant, the Holy Mountain (1,731ft/521m). The mountain is of geological interest, being a former volcanic vent, a great explosion cavity whose crater walls rose over a thousand feet. The road heads inland beyond Camas nan Geall and the easiest approach to the summit (there is no path) is from the high point on the road.

Just over a mile short of Kilchoan, a small road branches left towards the shore. Here, on a rocky plinth, stands Mingary Castle, a thirteenth-century fortress which was the stronghold of the MacIains for four hundred years. The castle has hexagonal curtain

---

◄ *The bay of Camas nan Geall, Ardnamurchan. Cladh Chiarain is marked to right of centre.*

Looking east to Beinn Resipol from the north shore of ► *Loch Sunart.*

The very old pillar in the graveyard of Cladh Chiarain. ► ►

walls with rounded corners, bounded by sea on three sides, and by an artificial channel cut from the basaltic rock on the remaining sides. During 1493 and 1495 James IV visited the castle and held court to accept the submission of several Highland chiefs.

The rocky bay close by the castle is known as Port nan Spainteach, "Bay of the Spaniards", taking its name from the hundred Spanish soldiers who gave assistance to Maclean of Duart after their galleon had sailed into Tobermory Bay, on Mull, to shelter from storms. In the year 1588, before laying siege to Mingary Castle, they put to the sword the occupants of Canna and Muck, sparing neither sex nor age. After three days Maclean gave up trying to take Mingary Castle and laid waste the land of Ardnamurchan instead. Before this incident, MacIain of Ardnamurchan had been the suitor of Duart's mother, and to further his own ends, Maclean had agreed to the union. After the ceremony, held on Mull, MacIain and his bride retired to their own chamber whilst his followers, having been well entertained by their hosts, went to sleep in a barn, but later in the night, all MacIain's men were murdered. MacIain heard their screams and was awake when Maclean entered the room with his men; his wife pleaded for his life. Tradition has it that he was tortured daily by the Macleans. During the early part of the seventeenth century the Clan Iain were making a nuisance of themselves, and were well established as pirates on the west coast. The tribe was then more or less annihilated by the Government, who appointed various chiefs to perform this task. The MacIains never really emerged again as a clan but became absorbed in the

◄ *Stone carvings in Cladh Chiarain.*

Rhum, Eigg and the Cuillin of Skye from the road to ►
Kilchoan, Ardnamurchan.

Mingary Castle, Ardnamurchan. ► ►

Clanranald. In 1644 the castle was taken for Montrose by Colkitto MacDonald, who held it during a siege from Argyll's army.

A little to the west of the castle is a pier used by the Tobermory-Kilchoan ferry. Kilchoan is a pleasant little village snuggling round a bay with fine views back to Ben Hiant and across to Mull where, in the early hours, the cliffs of Bloody Bay reflect the morning light.

To reach Ardnamurchan Point and Sanna Bay it is necessary to strike inland once again; from Kilchoan a narrow strip of tarmac takes one over the spine of Ardnamurchan, to descend through the ring dyke complex. This basin is known to geologists as "the Great Eucrite" and is the most remarkable ring dyke in Ardnamurchan. It forms a complete ring, one mile in annular width. These dykes are associated with volcanic activity and are formed by magma forcing its way, in ring formation, through the earth's crust.

Sanna Bay is one of the finest on the west coast of Scotland. In reality it is four bays, each separated by a small, rocky headland. Sanna is a crofting community and the people from Swordle, further to the east, were moved here to make way for sheep. On a good day it is worth scrambling up the rock peak of Meall Sanna which rises above the bay.

The road, fittingly narrow, ends at Ardnamurchan Point but you can walk from there to Sanna, following the coast and passing Portuairk, then Port na Cairidh where an old boathouse and a pier keep the Atlantic company. It is worth lingering along this shore where whales, sharks and porpoises can sometimes be spotted; there is good fishing too, of a less ambitious nature, for the average angler.

The granite-built lighthouse of Ardnamurchan stands solemnly 118ft high on its solid bedrock perch. It is open to the public at certain times and is

◄ *Kilchoan, with Ben Hiant beyond.*

worth visiting, even in bad weather. Ardnamurchan can be translated as both Point of the Sea Hounds and the Point of the Great Ocean. Either reading seems highly fitting to this most westerly point on the British mainland: twenty-three miles west of Land's End. More than a dozen islands can be seen from the point on a fine day and on that exposed stance the power of the ocean can be fully appreciated.

A side road continues from Kilmory as far as Ockle. Near Kilmory a narrow north-facing bay bites deeply into the rocky shore. The more exposed bay immediately to its east is where St. Columba landed and is reputed to have found and baptised bandits who were occupying a cave with two entrances close to high-water mark.

From here one can walk along the north shore of Ardnamurchan as far as Acharacle (there is a bus service between Acharacle and Kilchoan). There are numerous interesting coves and caves, some of which, near Ockle, have been explored by spelaeologists. The track runs from the road-end at Ockle, past the bay at Gortenfern, one of the finest in Ardnamurchan, to Kentra Bay, near Acharacle.

Acharacle is a useful centre for visiting the surrounding country, though the village itself has no particular merit. There is good fishing and walking and, during the summer months, a boat runs up Loch Shiel to Glenfinnan. There is a pleasant walk to Gortenfern along a forestry road and, in the other direction, a track takes one to Achnanellan. Beinn Resipol can be climbed from here; or, as an alternative approach, a boat may be hired at Dalelia, on Loch Shiel.

▲ ◄ *The Great Eucrite, Ardnamurchan, is a remarkable ring dyke, a mile in annular width. There are further ring dykes within this complex.* (Crown copyright reserved)

◄ *Sanna, from Meall Sanna.*

Ardtoe lies on the north side of Kentra Bay; there are many sandy inlets on this peninsula, each with a fine outlook towards Rhum and Eigg.

The tail of Loch Shiel tapers into the River Shiel near Acharacle and flows lazily into the Atlantic at the South Channel of Loch Moidart. Just past Shiel Bridge a road branches left and runs alongside the river to a beach close to Castle Tioram. This castle stands in splendid isolation on a tidal island. It belonged formerly to the MacDonalds of Clanranald and has had a chequered history. The structure is pentangular, cleverly grafted on the underlying crag, with high curtain walls, a damp dungeon and a turreted keep.

Tioram Castle was constructed in 1353 by Lady Anne MacRuari, whose husband was First Lord of the Isles. Though Tioram was never taken by siege it was cunningly captured by the Earl of Argyll. He had been ordered to harry Clanranald, so his galleys remained in the vicinity of the castle for five weeks. Part of this time he spent under the west walls; these seaward walls had no windows. Eventually he set sail for Ardnamurchan Point. This was merely a subterfuge, for as soon as Clanranald left the castle, Argyll returned and occupied the then deserted building.

When he heard the news, Clanranald summoned his clan and, returning to Tioram, massacred every Campbell there. The castle was finally burned by Clanranald himself when he left to fight for the Old Pretender; he knew that if he died in battle, the ancestral home of his clan would be taken over by the hated Campbells. Nowadays, Castle Tioram, with its setting of sand, sea and rocky headlands, is one of the finest in the west of Scotland.

◄ *Ardnamurchan lighthouse, the most westerly point on the British mainland.*

Moidart:
the Young Pretender and the funeral road to Dalelia

THIS COASTLINE IS rich in history, especially with the adventures of the Young Pretender, Prince Charles Edward Stuart. The Prince stayed several days, from August 11th to 17th, 1745, at Kinlochmoidart House which was once the seat of the MacDonalds. The clan was devoted to the Jacobite cause. A bodyguard of fifty Clanranald Highlanders went on foot from Glen Borrodale and watched over him whilst he planned his campaign which was to end so disastrously. After the Prince's defeat at Culloden, MacDonald of Kinlochmoidart was captured and hanged. His head was severed and placed in a prominent position above the gates of Carlisle, where it remained for many years: a grizzly warning to other aspiring revolutionaries. The Clan MacDonald of Kinlochmoidart – men, women and children – were also hunted by the Redcoats and many died. When Cumberland's men burned down the old house, they dragged the dangerously ailing mother of Kinlochmoidart out to the four great yew trees in the garden, under which they were encamped. The present house stands in fine wooded grounds but it is not open to the public.

In a field by the shore, a short distance south-east of the post office, stand seven beech trees. They are known as the Seven Men of Moidart and were planted to commemorate the seven men who accompanied Prince Charles Edward when he landed from France on July 25th, 1745: the Marquis of Tullibardine; Sir Thomas Sheridan, at one time the Prince's tutor; Sir John MacDonald; Francis Strickland, from England; Aeneas MacDonald, a brother of Kinlochmoidart and

---

◄ *Tioram Castle, Moidart.*

Kinlochmoidart House, where Prince Charlie stayed. ►

The Seven Men of Moidart. ► ►

at that time a banker in Paris; a clergyman called George Kelly and, lastly, a man in the French service, O'Sullivan. Two of the trees died and have since been replanted. The smallest one (third from left in the photograph) is said to have been planted by one of the men who was disloyal to the Prince.

Close by the bridge at the head of Loch Moidart a small road leads back up into the glen. It is possible to walk up the old funeral road which runs from Brunery past General Ross's Cairn, over the hill, to Loch Shiel. At Dalelia, on Loch Shiel, a boat may be hired to visit Eilean Fhionnan, the MacDonald Burial Isle, now usually called the Green Isle.

Eilean Fhionnan, like Glenfinnan, is named after St. Finnan who died in 575. A great number of pilgrims used to come to the island to visit his cell. The island is still used as a burial ground, though it is becoming somewhat crowded! The ruins of the church date back to the sixteenth century when it was built by Allan, Chief of Clanranald. Chained by the stone altar is a square bronze bell, one of seven still surviving in Scotland; it was stolen after the 'Forty-five by Redcoats, but later replaced. A tranquil atmosphere pervades Eilean Fhionnan; to its north-east the narrows of the loch cleave the hills on either side. A pair of eagles nest on a nearby peak, whilst blackcock may sometimes be seen on the island. In the eighteenth century there was a school on the island run by the most famous of Gaelic poets, Alexander Mac-Donald who later became a zealous Jacobite. He was born in the old Dalelia House (the present one was built by his grandson towards the end of the eighteenth century) and his gravestone lies on Eilean Fhionnan – on it, the carved figure of a skeleton – although, due to a severe storm, he was actually buried at Arisaig.

◄ *Looking from the old funeral road down Loch Moidart with Eigg in the distance.*

. . . the sea proclaimed peace with us
   At the fork of Islay Sound
And the hostile barking wind
   Was ordered off the ground.

It went to the upper places of the air
   And became a quiet
Glossy-white surface to us there
   After all its riot,
and to God we made thanksgiving
   That good Clanranald

Was spared the brutal death for which
   The elements had wrangled.
Then we pulled down the speckled canvas
   And lowered
The sleek red masts and along her bottom
   Safely stored,

And put out the slender well-wrought oars
   Coloured, and smooth to the hand,
Made of pine cut by Mac Bharais
   In St. Finnan's Island,
And set up the right-royal, rocking, rowing,
   Deft and timeous,

And made good harbour there at the top
   Of Carrick-Fergus.
We threw out anchors peacefully
   In that roadstead.
We took food and drink unstinting
   And there we stayed.

"The Voyage", Alexander MacDonald

◀ ◀ *Stone crosses on Eilean Fhionnan, Loch Shiel, Dalelia.*

◀ *The carved figure of a skeleton was intended as a*
gravestone for the celebrated Gaelic poet, the Reverend
Alexander MacDonald (Alasdair MacMhaghstir
Alasdair), Eilean Fhionnan. Due to a storm,
the poet was buried at Arisaig instead.

On his journey to Glenfinnan to raise the standard, Prince Charlie crossed over the funeral road to Dalelia, then travelled by boat up Loch Shiel to spend the night with MacDonald of Glenaladale. Next morning, accompanied by twenty-five men in three boats, he disembarked at the head of Loch Shiel where the river flows into the loch.

North of Loch Moidart, from Glenuig Bay, it is possible to continue westwards along the northern shore, by road and track, to the old crofting community of Smearisary. In fine weather the beach at Samalaman Bay offers excellent bathing.

At the entrance to Loch Ailort is Eilean nan Gobhar, where there are the ruins of a vitrified fort. Across the road from Roshven farm the westerly ridge of Rois Bheinn (2,892ft/882m) dips down to the road and this ridge offers a good means of ascent. From Rois Bheinn's summit the wide prospect of Arisaig and Moidart, with their jigsaw-like coastline, can be savoured in full.

◄ *Author examining stone altar and Celtic bronze bell in the church ruins on Eilean Fhionnan.*

Rois Bheinn, on the right, with An Stac on the road to Lochailort. ►

Looking across to the fish farm at Kinlochailort, Rois Bheinn in the distance, its west ridge running down right. ► ►

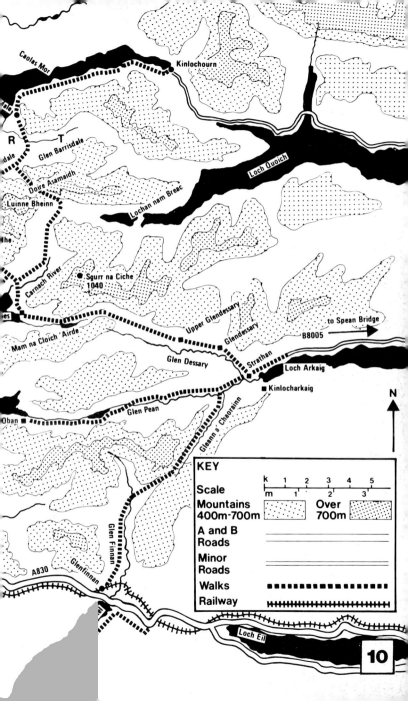

Arisaig and Morar:
Prince Charles Edward, Morag and Mallaig

THE RUGGED PENINSULA of Ardnish separates Loch Ailort from Loch nan Uamh (pronounced "Ooa"). Loch nan Uamh has both joyful and tragic connections with Prince Charles Edward: it was here that he landed in July 1745, and it was from here that he eventually departed, leaving behind a trail of sorrow and repercussions which were to have a profound effect on the lives of the Highlanders.

Rowans and oaks reach down to the margin of the shore; in summer, seals snooze on the rocks, whilst the cries of oyster catchers and curlews echo from the bays. The most famous of these bays is the Prince's Beach, where the Glen Borrodale burn meets the sea beside the point, Rubh'Ard Ghamhsgail. At the eastern end of this bay are the remains of an Iron Age vitrified fort which is one of four in the Sound of Arisaig.

When Charles came ashore on July 25th, he was accompanied by the "Seven Men"; stores were offloaded from the *Du Teilley* and she set sail again for France. The ship had been lying at anchor since the 19th, whilst the Prince held several conferences in a large tent erected on deck and which, a contemporary observer stated, was "furnished with a wide variety of wines and spirits". However, the Young Pretender had arrived without money, arms or troops, and he had a hard time persuading the canny Highlanders to assist him in a bid for the throne. But persuade them he certainly did.

◀ *The Prince's Beach, Arisaig, where the River Borrodale flows into Loch nan Uamh. To the left are the remains of an Iron Age vitrified fort (inset).*

Glen Borrodale House, where the Prince stayed for a ▶ *week after first landing in Arisaig. After its destruction by fire, the house was rebuilt to its original design.*

The sands of Morar. ▶ ▶

When Donald Cameron of Locheil heard that the Prince had come without arms and military support, he resolved to have no part in an uprising, considering the venture suicidal. But as the Prince had requested him to come to Borrodale House for conference, he decided to inform Prince Charles in person of his reasons for not giving his support. En route for Loch nan Uamh, Locheil called at his brother's house at Fassfern. It was early in the morning when the young chief arrived and John Cameron, his brother, asked him the reason for such an early visit. When he heard the full story, Fassfern applauded his brother's prudence in declining to take part in the Prince's schemes, but advised him to convey his sentiments by letter. "No," replied Locheil, "although my reasons admit of no reply, I ought at least to wait upon his Royal Highness." "Brother," answered Fassfern, "I know you better than you know yourself; if the Prince once sets eyes upon you, he will make you do whatever he pleases." Fassfern predicted correctly and the pledge of Donald Cameron of Locheil was a decisive factor, for at that time he held considerable sway over the West Highland clans.

Glen Borrodale House, where the Prince stayed, is the farmhouse close to the main road, about a quarter of a mile from the beach where he landed; the large mansion set on high ground across the way is Arisaig House.

The Prince remained a week at Glen Borrodale House as the guest of Angus MacDonald. After his defeat at Culloden he returned and was rowed by night through a severe storm to Benbecula in the Outer Hebrides. In the spring he returned again, still hoping for a ship to take him to France, but he found the house razed to the ground and his friend Angus

◄ *The Prince's Cairn where he left Scotland to board the French ship,* L'Heureux, *just after midnight on September 20th, 1746.*

MacDonald living in a rough shack close by. Though the area was seething with troops, he managed to evade them and slept in a nearby cave (Loch nan Uamh means "Loch of the Caves"), then he took to the mountains. Although there was a price of £30,000 on his head, he was not betrayed and he led the Redcoats a merry dance throughout the Highlands until September. He then returned yet again to Loch nan Uamh, having received intelligence that two French ships had arrived. With a number of friends he boarded *L'Heureux*, which set sail on Saturday, September 20th, 1746, thus ending a saga which, though appealing to the romantic, left misery and destruction in its wake. A signpost by the road indicates the point from which he finally left the shores of Scotland.

It was in Loch nan Uamh that a sea battle took place after Culloden between two French ships and three English frigates. The French ships had arrived rather late to help the Prince, carrying arms and 7,000 louis d'or. The money, together with some brandy, no doubt for medicinal purposes, was safely landed at Glen Borrodale, however, and after a skirmish with the frigates the French got clean away.

A series of sandy coves stretch beyond Arisaig; about a dozen in all nuzzle the sea coast as far north as the River Morar, offering delightful bathing in hot weather.

The sands of Morar are renowned, but unfortunately their unique beauty is now marred by the ubiquitous caravan. It is the Riviera of the west coast of Scotland and deservedly popular with holiday-makers. Across the Sound of Sleat, the Isle of Skye beckons invitingly. Loch Morar is twelve miles long and one of the deepest lochs in Europe at over 1,000 feet. Morag is the name of its resident monster: not much is heard of Morag but over the years many reliable sightings have been made, a high proportion by local inhabitants. Unlike Loch Ness, Loch Morar does not contain innumerable particles of peat obscuring the water, so it is possible to use closed circuit television cameras to obtain underwater pictures without auxiliary lighting. One can't help wondering whether it will be Loch Morar that provides the first scientifically acceptable photographs of an aquatic monster.

After the Prince's defeat in June 1746 at Culloden, Lord Lovat, a cunning and unprincipled character who only decided to support the Prince after his victory at Prestonpans, fled to the largest island at the western end of Loch Morar and hid there in a hollow tree. He was captured and executed the following year when he was eighty years old and so infirm that two warders had to help him mount the scaffold. The crush at his execution was so great that a number of spectators died when a scaffold collapsed. A wit to the last, Lovat remarked, "The more mischief, the better sport." He felt the edge of the executioner's axe and, approvingly, gave him a handsome donation. His head was severed in a single blow.

A road follows the north shore of Loch Morar for three miles and a track continues on to South Tarbet Bay where it is possible to strike northwards across the isthmus to Tarbet Bay on Loch Nevis where, on certain days, the Mallaig boat calls. Tarbet has one house, the post office, and a small church. The journey can, of course, be done in the other direction which may be more convenient. There is good fishing in Loch Morar and boats can be hired at Bracora. From Bracorina a hill track can be taken over to Stoul on the shore of Loch Nevis, passing en route Lochan a' Chuirn Duibh and Lochan Stole.

Monster hunters on Brinacory Island, Loch Morar, ▶
checking the underwater closed circuit television
monitoring camera.

The west end of Loch Morar. It was on the largest island ▶ ▶
that Lord Lovat hid after Culloden.

Mallaig is still essentially a fishing port, with large annual catches of herring and shellfish. There is bustling activity in the harbour, fish boxes are loaded on to the broad backs of waiting trucks amidst a forest of masts. A truly absorbing spectacle, though, as the industry becomes progressively more sophisticated, one cannot help wondering how long the fishing of these waters can continue.

From Mallaig itself a road follows the coast round into the jaws of Loch Nevis at Mallaigvaig. It was on June 5th, 1745, that Prince Charlie landed here from Elgol in Skye, after walking through Glen Sligachan in the Cuillin. From this crofting community a precipitous track leads on for a further half mile to Mallaigmore; it is known locally as "the Burma Road".

From Mallaig a car ferry runs to Armadale, in Skye; though more expensive than either the Kyle of Lochalsh or Kyle Rea ferry, it offers a good southerly approach to the Misty Isle, arriving more or less at the "foot" of the island. Steamers for the Outer Isles also leave from here, and there is a boat service four days a week to the Small Isles: Rhum, Eigg, Muck and Canna. There are many other opportunities to test your sea legs, including trips to Loch Scavaig, which allow a short time on shore to visit Loch Coruisk, and thrice weekly there are passenger services to Inverie in Knoydart, and Tarbet, Loch Nevis. During the summer the boat sometimes visits Camusrory at the head of Loch Nevis. From this lonely spot it is possible to take the old right of way to Loch Arkaig but, as with the walk from the head of Loch Morar which also takes one out at the west end of Loch Arkaig, there are problems, unless transport is arranged, in getting back to civilisation.

The scenery round Loch Nevis is most dramatic

◄ *The north shore of Loch Morar, left. The path to Tarbet follows the shore most of the way before cutting over to Loch Nevis. Ahead, Brinacory Island.*

and the boat trip to Tarbet a very worthwhile expedition. One of the most elegant peaks in the country, Sgurr na Ciche, dominates the head of the loch. Isolated dwellings on the north shore receive virtually no sunshine during the winter, as they are tucked under the shadow of high peaks stepping up steeply from the water.

No roads to Knoydart

KNOYDART IS BOUNDED on the south by Loch Nevis and to the north by Loch Hourn. From a landward direction this is one of the most remote areas of the British mainland, yet it is readily accessible by sea from Mallaig. No highways reach into Knoydart but there are several estate roads around Inverie, used by local people.

From Inverie, continuing round Inverie Bay, a path leads west, then north, past long-forsaken crofts where the narrow trenched strips of once cultivated lazybeds can still be seen under their cover of turf and bracken.

It is possible to visit Inverie for a few hours between boat schedules and return to Mallaig via Tarbet the same day. This allows enough time for a short trek in Knoydart and also gives the opportunity of a glimpse into inner Loch Nevis; those so inclined could finish the day off walking back from Tarbet to Loch Morar and the road-end, provided that transport is arranged at the other end. There is a post office at Inverie and now a hostel, run by Knoydart Estate, for those wishing to stay overnight. The only other alternative is to camp.

◄ *Buyers on the quay at Mallaig.*

Weekend rest. Fishing boats at Mallaig. ►

Tarbet, Loch Nevis. Mail and passengers going ashore. ► ►
The house behind is the post office.

There are several more ambitious fine walks from Inverie; two glens reach into the mountains from this scattering of houses. The main track goes up Gleann an Dubh Lochain, over Mam Barrisdale to Barrisdale on Loch Hourn. From here it is possible to cross to Arnisdale on the north shore of Loch Hourn by the mail boat. The peaks of Luinne Bheinn and Meall Bhuidhe – both over 3,000ft (900m) – can be ascended from Dubh Lochain. Alternatively, the very energetic can walk from Barrisdale through to Kinlochourn. It is a path which never strays far from the south shore of the loch, though it rises and falls abruptly over several spurs. Nearer Kinlochourn it takes the form of a man-made, rocky shelf a little above high water mark.

In Gleann an Dubh Lochain, just past the conspicuous memorial (Torr a' Bhalbhain) a path forks right to Gleann Meadail. It toils up Mam Meadail (1,800ft/548m), then drops down to the head of Loch Nevis. Here the Carnach River is dangerous to cross and should only be forded at its mouth during low tide. In summer, on certain days it may be possible to catch a boat back from Camusrory to Mallaig. Enquiries should be made in Mallaig, before setting out, as it is no longer a regular service. Should transport by boat be available to Camusrory a further walk is possible keeping to the west side of the River Carnach. Beyond the small ruin by a superb pool the path vanishes, but continue, bearing slightly left to gain the Lochan nam Breac/Barrisdale path which cuts across the head of the valley high up. After passing through Doire Asamaidh the descent is made to Barrisdale.

◄ *Looking past Loch Nevis narrows, Kyleknoydart, to Sgurr na Ciche.*

A fishing boat heads into Loch Nevis. In the background ►
is the south coast of Knoydart.

Inverie with Sgurr Coire Choineachain behind. ► ►

Ladhar Bheinn (3,343ft/1010m), meaning "Forked Mountain", can be climbed from Gleann na Guiserein, a wide open glen which runs westwards from Ladhar Bheinn to the sea. A forestry road leads into this glen via the Mam Uidhe, to the north of Inverie. The right-hand branch of the road leads high into Gleann na Guiserein to the bottom of the long slope up to the top of Ladhar Bheinn. From the top there are superb vistas on a good day, whilst its northern corrie is one of the finest and wildest on the western seaboard.

Glenfinnan, Loch Arkaig, Glen Dessary

THE ACTUAL SITE of the raising of the standard in Glenfinnan was probably where the Roman Catholic church now stands. It was on August 19th, 1745, at eleven a.m., that the Prince arrived after spending the night with Glenaladale. He was bitterly disappointed, for he expected to see a large number of clansmen and there were only a few locals to greet him. It was not until one p.m. that a pibroch was heard and his spirits rose at the sight of between seven and eight hundred Camerons "all plaided and plumed in their tartan array" arriving in two columns, each three men deep. The Bratach Bhan – the Stewart banner of white and crimson silk – was blessed by Bishop Hugh MacDonald and raised by William Murray, the Duke of Atholl, amidst a frenzy of pipes and skimmering bonnets. By late evening twelve hundred men were

---

◄ *The memorial in Gleann an Dubh Lochain, Knoydart.*

Looking up Gleann Meadail to Sgurr na Ciche beyond. ►
The path up this glen branches just beyond the memorial, left. The Loch Hourn track continues up Gleann an Dubh Lochain, to the left.

The head of Loch Shiel and the 'Forty-five monument. ► ►
The standard was raised where the Roman Catholic church, right, now stands. The building in the foreground was probably used as the armoury.

encamped and O'Sullivan was appointed quartermaster. Tradition has it that the old house across the main road from the Roman Catholic church was used as the armoury. For better or worse, the rebellion was under way.

About one and a half miles east of the head of Loch Shiel a forestry road leads to the east side of Loch Shiel and though motor vehicles are not permitted to use this, it can provide a pleasant and easy walk along the loch shore. The road continues all the way to Polloch in Sunart where it joins up with the public road to Strontian.

Loch Arkaig lies to the north and west of Fort William. It can be approached either from the Mallaig direction, by turning off before the Caledonian Canal bridge at Banavie, or by travelling through Spean Bridge and taking the left fork at the Commando Memorial. Achnacarry, the seat of the Camerons of Locheil, is passed on the left before reaching the Dark Mile, a dense avenue of trees, mainly planes, which still seem to hide secrets of the past in their shadows. The avenue holds but a fraction of its former glory now, marred by thinning and the depredation of time. At the far end of the Dark Mile, the road passes over a burn which cascades down from Gleann Cia-aig in spectacular falls. During his widespread wanderings in the autumn of 1746, Prince Charles lived in a cave above these falls, and reputedly

◄ *Looking down Loch Shiel from Glenfinnan. A forest road (no cars) goes down the south-east shore, left, starting 2 km along the Fort William road.*

From the head of Loch Eil a narrow road follows the south shore, then runs down the west shore of Loch Linnhe to Corran ferry. En route there are very good views of Ben Nevis. ►

Neptune's Staircase. At the Caledonian Canal bridge, Banavie, near Fort William. Ben Nevis is in the background. ► ►

UNITED · WE · CONQUER

IN MEMORY OF
THE OFFICERS AND
MEN OF
THE COMMANDOS
WHO DIED IN THE
SECOND WORLD WAR
1939 1945
THIS COUNTRY WAS
THEIR TRAINING
GROUND

took refuge in at least one hollow tree – a doubtful tale.

The road follows the northern margin of Loch Arkaig, but on both sides there are remnants of the forest of Caledon, oaks and pines, perhaps some of the oldest trees in Scotland. Boats were at one time used extensively for transport on the loch and the skeletal remains of old piers are still to be seen. It is twelve miles up to Strathan at the head of the loch and for the last mile the road is unsurfaced. The road then forks and becomes either a rough track or a forestry road.

The right-hand branch of the road continues up Glen Dessary to the cottage of Upper Glendessary and from there a track is found on the uphill side of the cottage. It is eight miles from the head of Loch Arkaig to Sourlies on Loch Nevis. The route climbs over Mam na Cloich'Airde, the Pass of the High Rock (1,000ft), and skirts below Sgurr na Ciche (3,410ft/1040m), the highest peak in Knoydart. It is possible to reach Knoydart via Gleann Meadail but the fording of the River Carnach (as mentioned earlier) is dangerous and should only be attempted at the mouth at low tide. The through route to Knoydart is only recommended for experienced walkers, although it is interesting to note that Roy's six-inch map of 1755 marks this route as a second-class road! On certain days during the summer months, tour boats visit Camusrory; enquiries about trips should be made in Mallaig.

It is difficult to believe that two hundred fighting men were recruited from Glen Dessary for the 'Forty-

◄ *The Commando Memorial near Spean Bridge. The Commando School during the Second World War was based at Achnacarry, the seat of Clan Cameron. One of the roads to Loch Arkaig runs from here.*

Looking westwards up Loch Arkaig. ►

Glen Dessary. Looking over Lochan a' Mhaim and Mam na ► ► *Cloich Airde to Loch Nevis beyond.*

five. They were led to Glenfinnan by Miss Jenny Cameron who rode at the head of the clansmen. All that remains in this lonely glen now are two houses – Glendessary, Upper Glendessary, a bothy, the wild deer, and a pair of eagles which nest in the lower glen.

The left-hand branch of the road at Strathan leads down across the River Dessary where a new forestry road extends into Glen Pean. On the left is Gleann a'Chaorainn which leads through to Glenfinnan. Until relatively recently, a housewife living at the cottage of Strathan walked once a month to Glenfinnan and from there took the train to Fort William to do her shopping. She returned to Strathan the same night, again tackling the eight-mile walk, complete with groceries! After Culloden Prince Charles and three followers spent the night with Donald Cameron at Kinlocharkaig. The path leading through to Oban on Loch Morar is more boggy than that through Glen Dessary. You should cross the River Pean at Pean bothy and follow the south side of the glen to the head of Loch Morar. This was the route which the Prince took to reach Glen Borrodale House. A hoard of 37,000 louis d'or, possibly originating from the two French frigates and intended to help the Young Pretender's cause, is supposed to have been buried close to the west end of Loch Arkaig. The money was contained in seven barrels. A Lochaber man was reputed to have discovered part of the hoard at the turn of the century but he has remained prudently anonymous and never disclosed the whereabouts of his find.

◄ *The junction of the paths at the west end of Loch Arkaig. To the right is Glen Dessary, in the centre, Glen Pean. To the left is Gleann a'Chaorainn, which leads to Glenfinnan. Streap is the peak to the left of this glen.*

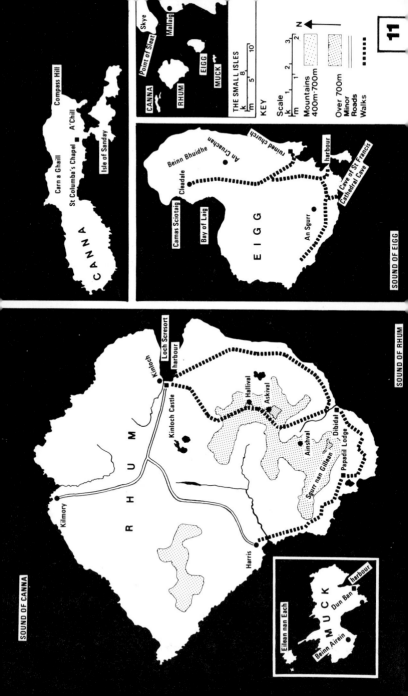

SOUND OF CANNA

SOUND OF RHUM

RHUM

Kilmory

Kinloch

Loch Scresort

harbour

Kinloch Castle

Hallival

Askival

Ainshval

Sgurr nan Gillean

Oidhal

Papadil Lodge

Harris

Eilean nan Each

MUCK

Dun Ban

Benn Airein

harbour

CANNA

Carn a Ghaill

Compass Hill

St Columba's Chapel

A'Chill

Isle of Sanday

THE SMALL ISLES

CANNA

RHUM

EIGG

MUCK

Point of Sleat

Skye

Mallaig

KEY

Scale

Mountains
400m–700m

Minor
Roads

Over 700m

Walks

11

N

EIGG

SOUND OF EIGG

Beinn Bhuidhe

An Cruachan

ruined church

Cleadale

Camas Sciotaig

Bay of Laig

An Sgurr

Cave of St Francis

Cathedral Cave

harbour

The Small Isles:
Canna, Rhum, Eigg and Muck

THE PARISH OF the Small Isles comprises Canna, Rhum, Eigg and Muck. There are four sailings a week from Mallaig to these Isles (not always calling at Muck, so visitors must disembark at Eigg and arrange private transport). Even the day trip is well worthwhile and relatively inexpensive. The boat sails on Monday, Wednesday, Thursday and Saturday.

Canna harbour, the deepest in the Small Isles, displays well-autographed rock faces by the jetty: the work of bored mariners, no doubt. Two and a half miles west of the harbour are the ruins of a convent and a stone cross stands at A'Chill, near the ruins of St. Columba's Chapel. Compass Hill (458ft), so called because it deflects the compass, rises from the east coast of the island. Bands of columnar dolerite sandwiched between bedded conglomerates are exposed in the cliffs, offering a superb section for geological study. As well as basalt, the deposits contain pieces of charred wood and plants. Carn a Ghaill (690ft/210m) is the highest hill on the island, while a bridge connects Canna with the Isle of Sanday. The west point of Canna, like the Sgurr of Eigg, is fortified by a wall; a small sea stack, lying quarter of a mile north of the harbour, is where a Chief of Clanranald once imprisoned his wife.

For a long time the Abbey of Iona had jurisdiction over the Island of **Muck** and one theory is that its name derives from Monk Island. However, the Gaelic form is Eilean-nan-Muchd (Island of the Swine). The highest hill on the island is Beinn Airein (451ft/138m). There is a guest house under construction and also several cottages which can be rented. Most of the island is composed of sheet basalt with many dolerite dykes. Dun Ban, overlooking the harbour entrance of Muck, is a Bronze Age fortification. Muck and Canna

both enjoy a relatively mild climate, allowing the production of early potatoes by the end of May.

Rhum, or to be more correct, Rum, is an island of 26,400 acres and is the most barren of the Small Isles. It was purchased in 1957 by the Nature Conservancy Council from the Trustees of the late Sir George Bullough. Kinloch is the only centre of population. About forty people live there and, with the exception of the school teacher, all are employed by the Nature Conservancy.

Sir George built Kinloch Castle at the turn of the century, employing kilted Welsh stone-masons to construct the 150-foot square building from Arran sandstone. Its heyday lasted but twelve years, during which time there was employment for fourteen gardeners and twenty-four house staff. Alligators gambolled in heated pools and a brass piped orchestrion churned out a repertoire of popular tunes. An exotic bath with a control panel like that of a battleship ensured that guests were both cleansed and amused. The castle and its contents are still intact and provide a unique insight to a way of life now gone. The building is reputed to have cost £250,000 to build. In those days casual visitors to the island were unwelcome; even today there are restrictions and there is virtually no accommodation except for visiting scientists – or experienced mountaineers who must camp. Day visitors are free to land at Loch Scresort and visit the places of interest round Kinloch. The castle can only be viewed by special arrangement and for a longer stay on the island, permission must be obtained from the Nature Conservancy Council, 63 Academy Street, Inverness. Rhum is one of the wetter islands. Harris averages 50ins of rain per year, Kinloch 87ins and in the lee of the peaks it is 120ins. Also gale-force winds have been recorded on eighteen days out of thirty-one. No doubt the wind

◄ *Canna.*

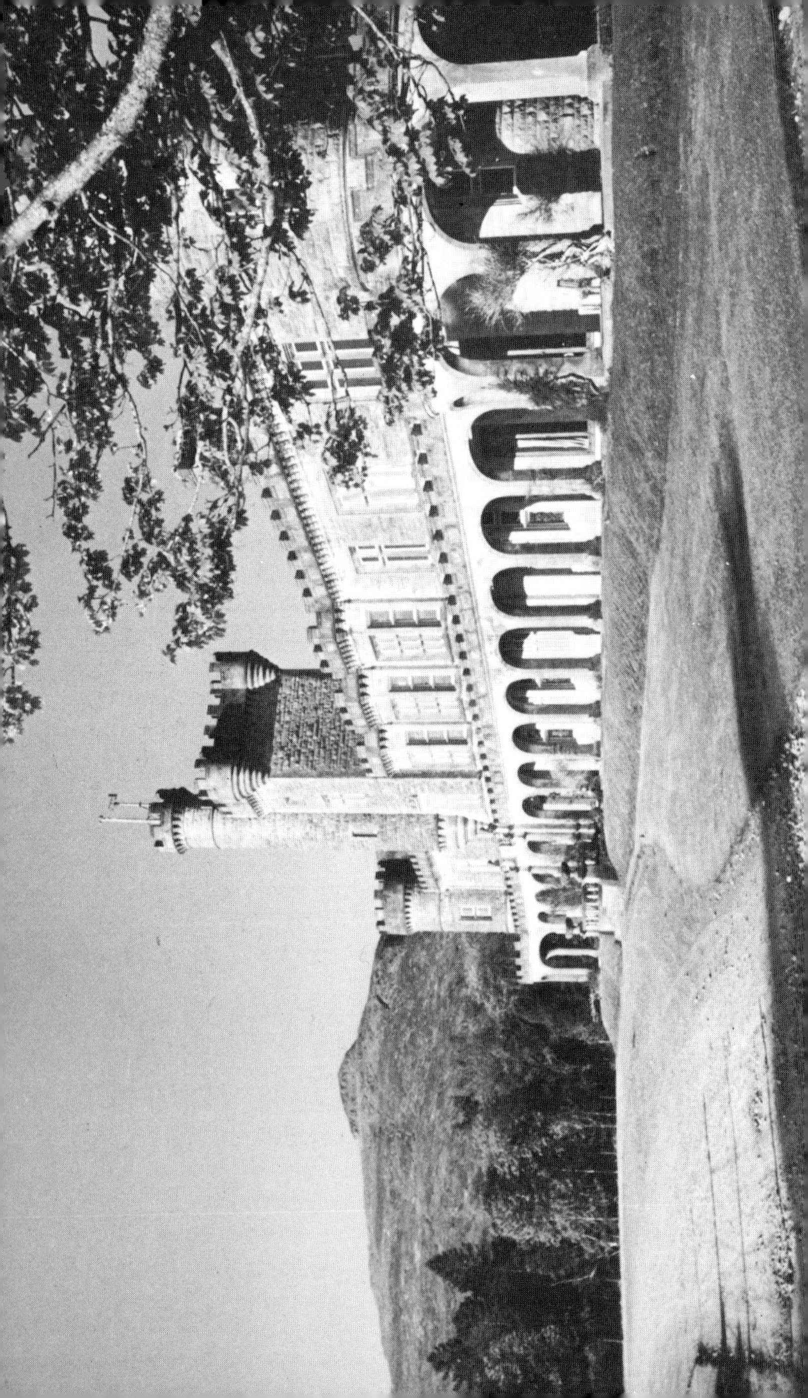

was good accompaniment for the Kinloch Castle organ. Dr. John McCulloch, a nineteenth-century geologist and traveller in the Western Isles, must have had weather, clegs and the voracious midge in mind when he described Rhum as "the most repulsive of all islands". Certainly the prolific tick is one of the less welcome and long-lasting souvenirs visitors can take away with them. The island is, however, of considerable interest geologically and consists of a frame of Torridonian sandstone, which is severed on the south-west by the sea and partially encompasses the root of a giant tertiary volcano.

The only roads on the island lead to Harris in the west and Kilmory in the north. Everywhere else access is by shank's pony and good paths lead round the coastline, offering superb clifftop views (weather permitting) of the islands and the mainland. The Hallival-Askival ridge walk provides an airy scramble for fitter visitors, which can be rounded off by descending to Dibidal on the east coast, where there is a bothy, and thence back to Kinloch by the coast path. Alternatively, a longer route can be taken by dropping to the west to Harris with the prospect of a tedious walk back along the rough road to Kinloch, if a courtesy lift in a Conservancy Land Rover is not available.

There is a fund of wild life and some of the deer meandering along the shore at Kinloch are extremely sociable. At Harris, which at one time was the area of greatest population, there is a herd of Highland cattle. The Rhum ponies, which are used for a variety of jobs on the island including carrying culled deer, are reputed to be descended from horses which swam ashore from wrecked ships of the Spanish Armada. They are fine sturdy beasts, some chestnut with silver

◀ *Kinloch Castle, Rhum.*

The Cuillin of Rhum from the Mausoleum at Harris. ▶

The Cuillin of Rhum. ▶ ▶

manes and tails, never standing more than fourteen hands. These can usually be seen at Kinloch. Rhum is the home of the golden eagle and now also the sea eagle, which has been reintroduced from Norway.

Eigg is an idyllic island, with a distinctive individual charm and a much drier climate than the adjoining mainland. There is accommodation at Laig farm and there are cottages and caravans to let. Cars can sometimes be hired, though driving is limited; certainly the roads are not overburdened with traffic! Information for accommodation can be obtained from the Tourist officer, Eigg Estate (Mallaig 82428).

The Gaelic name for the island is Eilean Eige: the Isle of the Notch. Indeed, viewed from the north-west, the island does appear notched in the middle by a glen which divides it into two small mountain groups. The Sgurr dominates the island and is the highest point (1,289ft/393m), protruding like a hippo-potamus horn from the lava plateau, and almost completely encircled by cliffs; the 450ft overhanging nose, like the rest of the Sgurr, is composed of a sheet of columnar pitchstone. There are still remnants of an old fortified well at the Sgurr's westerly extremity and here golden rod, thyme, campion and giant heather grow profusely. Viewed from the south, where there is the greatest exposure of cliff, a long heathery ledge cutting across the escarpment is conspicuous; most of the rock climbs start from this point. A fossilised, coniferous tree can be seen on this same ledge.

◄ *A rock pinnacle, Orval, Rhum. The island left is Canna, with Compass Hill on the right.*

The Sgurr of Eigg from the east. The area in the foreground is a lava plateau and the Sgurr itself is formed from a great sheet of columnar pitchstone. ►

The ruins of the fortifications on the west end of An Sgurr. Rhum to the left, in the distance the Isle of Skye. ► ►

St. Donnan is the patron saint of the island, and also of Eilean Donnan in Kintail. As a missionary of St. Columba, he established a monastery on Eigg and was later murdered (circa 616) with fifty-two of his followers. At that time, before the Viking invasions, pirates were numerous throughout the Western Isles and it has been suggested that the queen of the country, angered by the presence of St. Donnan and his monks, instigated the massacre and hired pirates to perform the dastardly deed. Not far from the harbour, on the east side of the island, is a ruined church dedicated to the saint. About twenty yards from the church, a sepulchral urn was found by Martin Martin in the early eighteen century, which contained a number of headless skeletons.

In the south-east there are two famous caves, the Cathedral Cave, which was used for Roman Catholic services after the 'Forty-five and the Cave of Francis, where the MacLeods killed 395 MacDonalds by suffocating them. Several reasons are offered for the massacre of the MacDonalds, the most likely one being that it followed an incident when some of the MacLeods staying on the island became too amorous with the local maidens, and were subsequently bound and cast adrift in the Minch.

With mischief in mind, the MacLeods arrived on Eigg in the spring of 1577; deep snow covered the ground (nowadays a rare occurrence on the island). There was not a soul to be seen, since the populace, having sighted the invaders, had retired to the cave whose tiny entrance is shrouded beneath a waterfall. A strong wind covered their footprints with freshly

◄ *The Sgurr of Eigg from the south.*

The ruins of the five-hundred-year-old Kildonan church, ►
Eigg. A stone on the north wall is inscribed with the arms of Clan Ranald dated 1441.

The Cathedral Cave, Eigg. ► ►

fallen snow. After a thorough but fruitless search, the MacLeods set sail again in their galleys, temporarily frustrated in their objective. However a MacDonald rashly climbed on to a promontory to watch their departure and was spotted. The MacLeods returned and were able to follow his prints back to the cave as it had stopped snowing and the wind had dropped. The MacLeods diverted the stream, piled thatch and roof timbers from nearby crofts at the cave mouth and fired it, damping the flames and thereby asphixiating everyone inside. Several centuries later the bones of those who perished were gathered together and reverently interred. Only one family escaped the massacre because they had taken refuge in a different cave.

The two caves are found a mile to the south of the pier. To reach them, take the route up the hill as for the Sgurr. Then climb the first stile on the left. Continue along a path to a cottage, then by a sheep track to the cliff fence. Follow down a zig-zag path to the shore, close to a small burn. On the right is the Cathedral Cave and to the left, the Cave of Francis.

Eigg is an unforgettable island, rich both in flowers and history. The north and south of the island alike offer fine walks enabling one, at the end of the day, to drop down to the shoreline which is enhanced by many attractive sandy beaches. There is, for example, a good walk up the northerly backbone from An Cruachan to Beinn Bhuidhe, with a descent at the far end to a westward path, returning past the gleaming white Singing Sands (Camas Sciotaig). These sands sound like an Aeolian harp but only sing when dry and during temperature fluctuations. Here, at Cleadale, is the largest crofting community of the island. The shop, manse, doctor's house and church are built in approximately the centre of the island.

The Great Glen and ways west:
the Battle of the Shirts and the Loch Ness Monster

THE GREAT GLEN Fault which runs from Loch Linnhe to Inverness is a unique geological feature. The whole area of country to the north of the Great Glen is displaced sixty-five miles to the south-west, relative to the southerly section. This fault and, further south, the Highland Boundary Fault, are the two most notable lines of seismic activity in Britain. The construction of the Caledonian Canal, which connects the Atlantic Ocean to the North Sea through the Great Glen, was started by Thomas Telford in 1803 and took nineteen years to complete. The canal sections are linked by three lochs, Lochy, Oich and Ness. There is a total of twenty-two miles of canal with twenty-eight locks, and the lochs account for a further forty-five miles of waterway.

In 1544, at the north-eastern end of Loch Lochy, the Battle of the Shirts was fought between the Mac-Donalds and the Frasers. The fight took place on a blazing July day about noon and the combatants set to, clad only in kilts and shirts. By all accounts it was a bloody encounter; a contemporary report states: "They were felled down on each side like trees in a wood till room was made by these breaches and at last all came to fight hand and fist." Eventually Lord Lovat (Fraser), who had been cutting paths through his opponents with his two-handed sword, fell covered in wounds and the cry went up, "*Thuit an cruaidh chascar*" (The lusty slasher is fallen). Soon afterwards it was all over. It is recorded that only one of the Frasers escaped, but probably quite a few survived.

The Well of the Seven Heads is found on the western shore of Loch Oich and commemorates the place where, in the early part of the sixteenth century, the heads of seven murdered men were washed in a

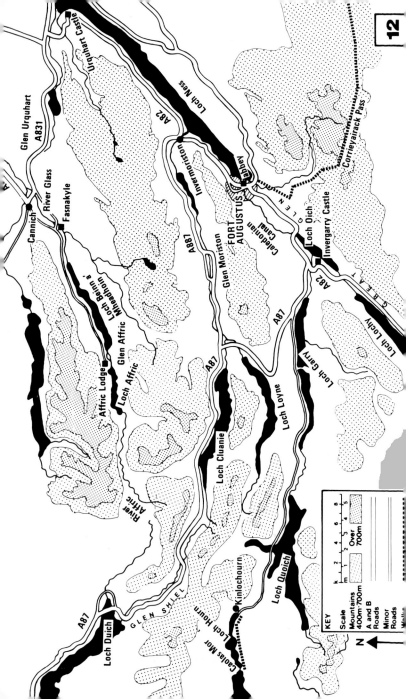

KEY

Scale

| Mountains 400m-700m | | Over 700m |

A and B Roads

Minor Roads

Walls

N

Glen Urquhart A831
River Glass
Cannich
Fasnakyle
Urquhart Castle
A82
Loch Ness
Invermoriston
Glen Urquhart

Abbey
FORT AUGUSTUS
Caledonian Canal
Glen Moriston
A887
Loch Oich
Invergarry Castle
Corrieyairack Pass
GLEN
GREAT
A82
Loch Lochy

Loch Beinn a' Mheadhoin
Affric Lodge
Glen Affric
Loch Affric
River Affric

A87
Loch Cluanie
Loch Loyne
Loch Garry

Kinlochourn
Caolas Mor
Loch Hourn
GLEN SHIEL
Loch Duich
A87
Loch Quoich

spring. The "beardless bard" Ian Lom, who later was to guide Montrose over the mountains on his famous mid-winter forced march to Inverlochy Castle, was the man who engineered their deaths as a reprisal for previous murders. The seven men were his own brother-in-law and six sons. Their heads, after being washed were placed at the feet of Glengarry in Glengarry Castle. They were buried in a small glade not far from Invergarry Mansion, now a hotel. In more recent times the bodies of seven men were dug up in Glen Spean. The skeletons were complete except for the skulls.

Creagan Fhitich – the Rock of the Raven – is where Invergarry Castle, of the MacDonell, was built. It is situated near the road on the bank of the Loch Oich, close to Glengarry Castle Hotel. The Duke of Cumberland set fire to the castle because the Prince and his followers had slept there before and after the Battle of Culloden.

Fort Augustus, still known to Gaelic speakers as Cill Chuimein, was originally named after St. Cummein, a follower of St. Columba. St. Columba himself stayed here whilst travelling to Inverness, which was the Pictish capital. Following the Battle of Killiecrankie in 1715, the English Government took over the ancient fort at the rear of the present day Lovat Arms Hotel. A short time later, when General Wade's road-building programme was in top gear, a much larger fort was under construction, close to the loch.

The Duke of Cumberland made Fort Augustus his headquarters after the 'Forty-five and revelled in all sorts of excesses. Many innocent people were put to

---

Invergarry Castle which was burned down by the "Bloody Butcher", the Duke of Cumberland after the 'Forty-five. ▶

The locks at Fort Augustus. The route over the Corrieyairack Pass begins behind the Abbey turrets, right. ▶ ▶

the sword, the countryside laid waste and their stock confiscated. More than 8,000 head of cattle were taken to Fort Augustus, sometimes as many as 2,000 in a single drove. Cumberland also promoted bare-back races on horseback for naked women and there is reference to the "old, buff Ladies" being successful. Major Wolfe (later General Wolfe, hero of Quebec) then under the command of the duke, considered these debauches deplorable: "If I stay here much longer with the regiment, I shall be perfectly corrupt: the officers are loose and profligate, and the soldiers are very devils."

In 1876 the fort was presented by Lord Lovat for use as a monastery and part of the ancient fort was incorporated into the new monastery building. It became an abbey in 1882 and the Abbey School is now widely known. Visitors are permitted to enter the precincts, where there is a museum. During the last century a large and colourful character ran this museum. He was George Gordon-Cumming, a well-known big-game hunter. His dress was eccentric and, even on visits to Edinburgh, he wore a Gordon tartan kilt and plaid fastened by a huge brooch, a brass helmet, jewellery, a frilly shirt and top boots. The ensemble was completed by silver fish hooks dangling from his ears.

The origin of that renowned body, the Ordnance Survey, can be traced to Fort Augustus. The Duke of Cumberland ordered his quartermaster, General Watson, and William Roy to set about mapping the countryside. Those early maps were never published but Roy continued with his work which eventually covered the whole of the Highlands.

Running south-east from Fort Augustus is a General Wade road. This is the famous Corrieyairack Pass (2,507ft/764m) which was crossed by Prince Charlie, who put on a new pair of brogues for the journey. To the south-west of this same pass went Montrose on his forced march to Inverlochy Castle.

Urquhart Castle is built on a promontory on the south side of Urquhart Bay. The old vitrified fort, which occupied the highest part of the castle precincts, may even have been intact when St. Columba visited it. The site commands a superb position with views stretching almost the full extent of the loch. Its Gaelic name is Caisteal-na-Stroine: the Castle of the Nose. It is reputed to have been in existence during the reign of William the Lion (1165–1214). Edward I came as far north as Elgin in 1296 and from there sent forces to capture the main strongholds of the north. Castle Urquhart was one so occupied, and it was to change hands several times before Bruce captured it around 1308. In 1313 he gave it over to the Earl of Moray, Sir Thomas Randolph. The building continued to have a violent history. By 1479 the destruction of the castle was almost complete and Glen Urquhart itself was laid waste. In 1509 the Lordship of Urquhart was gifted to the Red Bard, John Grant of Freuhie, with instructions to rebuild the castle. After the Battle of Flodden in 1513, the new Lord of the Isles, Sir Donald MacDonald of Lochalsh, again put the glen to fire and sword and took the castle. In fact, it was not until the seventeenth century that the major reconstruction of the castle was completed by the Grants. Several distinct modes of building can still be discerned, from the early Iron Age fort to the last stages of Grant's reconstruction in 1623. In 1715 it was reported that "the Castell of Urquhart is blowen down with the last storme of wind, the south-west side thereoff to the laich woult." This statement most likely refers to the keep, the south side of which has disappeared. The castle is now under the care of the Department of the Environment.

Probably the first recorded sighting of the Loch Ness Monster was made in the time of St. Columba. One of his monks had a narrow and miraculous

escape. In early times the monster was known by the local people as An Niseag, which means Water Horse. One of the deepest parts of the loch (975ft) lies close to Urquhart Castle and, though not as deep as Loch Morar, it is still one of the deepest lochs in Europe. Occupants of the castle's dungeon used to report hearing strange noises beneath their prison. According to legend, there is an underwater cavern which extends beneath the castle. There is certainly an abundant supply of fish in Loch Ness; eels have been caught up to six foot in length, and submarine crews have seen white eels at a depth of 900ft, so there is no shortage of food for a large aquatic beast.

After a sighting in 1933 the press christened the monster Nessie. The creature has been seen by countless witnesses over the years, some of the most reliable sightings having been made by monks at the abbey of Fort Augustus. Anyone taking the trouble to study these reports cannot fail to reach the conclusion that such a creature, or creatures, must exist. An interesting aspect of the reports is that Nessie has never been heard to make a noise, other than the surreptitious gurgle of water as it vanishes once again into obscurity. There also seems to be firm evidence for the belief that the monster is amphibious. At one time it was reported that the creature came ashore at Urquhart Bay. Nessie, or Nessies, since it appears that there may be a small clan of them, are described as being large – up to fifty-five feet long – with a small tapering head set on a neck about six foot in length. One of the best photographs of Nessie was taken in 1934 by a London surgeon. Nessie even made war news: in the early stages of the last war, an Italian newspaper reported that Nessie had been "liquidated" by an aerial bomb!

◄ *Urquhart Castle, Loch Ness. A view from the motte, which was the site of an early vitrified fort, looking to the nether bailey and tower.*

The temperature of the lower water in the loch remains almost static, at 5° C, and recent sonar expeditions have established that there are deep underwater fissures. During 1952 John Cobb met his death on Loch Ness whilst attempting to break the world water-speed record. His boat, the *Crusader*, hit what was reported as a patch of turbulence in the loch, not far from Urquhart Castle . . .

Recently there has been renewed interest in the search for the so-called monster; it seems a pity that most of the initiative has come from overseas. With an increased use of sonar apparatus and various types of underwater cameras, the secret of Loch Ness could be finally resolved within the next few years.

Glen Affric has always been a favourite Highland glen for tourists. From Cannich the road follows the River Glass for two miles to Fasnakyle. Here is the power station for the Glen Affric hydro-electric scheme and here, too, a somewhat bedraggled Prince Charlie lived in a cave with the Seven Men of Glenmoriston after his defeat at Culloden. Their standard of values was typical of Highlanders in those warlike days. One of the group went to a village and purchased what was, to them, a luxury of the highest order: a pennyworth of gingerbread. Their royal companion had a price of a mere £30,000 on his head!

From the western end of Loch Beinn a' Mheadhoin, a private road leads to Affric Lodge. This is fine walking country of outstanding beauty, with a wealth of good forestry roads and tracks.

The road to Kinlochourn branches off the Invergarry – Cluanie road and follows the north shore of Loch Garry, then past Loch Quoich and down a steep

◄ *Loch Affric and Affric Lodge.*

Glen Affric, Loch Beinn a'Mheadhoin. ►

Looking down on Loch Garry. The Kinlochourn road ► ►
follows the near shore.

brae to the road-end at Kinlochourn. As mentioned on page 175, the track from Inverie and Barrisdale ends at Kinlochourn. It is well worth walking down the good track on the south side of Loch Hourn for a way to obtain fine views west towards the narrows of Caolas Mor, and see the massif of Ladhar Bheinn rising majestically further down on the left. It is truly magnificent country and difficult to rival anywhere in the world.

Kintail:
Eilean Donnan, the Five Sisters
and the Falls of Glomach

KINTAIL HAS HAD a turbulent history by any Highland standards. It is the land of the MacKenzies and their castle, Eilean Donnan, is one of the most famous landmarks in the breadth of the Highlands, though their chief seat was at Brahan Castle near Beauly, across on the east coast.

Eilean Donnan Castle appears in isolated splendour at the meeting of the three lochs – Loch Long, Loch Duich and Loch Alsh. It is best seen against the background of the setting sun which turns the water of Loch Alsh a glorious red. Loch Duich is named after an eleventh-century saint, St. Dubhthach, but Eilean Donnan Castle was built on St. Donnan's Isle. It was he who founded a monastery on the island of Eigg in 616 and was massacred there, together with fifty-two followers.

The castle was built 700 years ago on the site of an earlier vitrified fort, part of which can still be seen today. The early castle was surrounded by water, but it is now linked to the shore by a causeway. Colin

◄ *Loch Hourn from close to the Kinlochourn – Barrisdale path. Ladhar Bheinn is the peak on the left.*

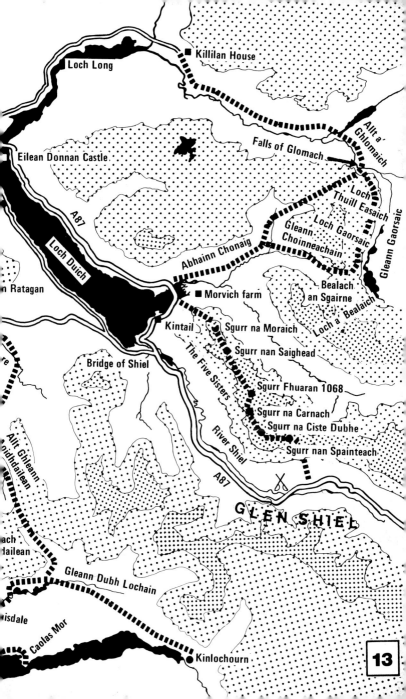

Fitzgerald was made constable of the castle by Alexander III after displaying outstanding bravery at the Battle of Largs in 1263 (where Haco's Norsemen were defeated). It is from Colin that the Clan MacKenzie are descended.

Eilean Donnan Castle was to change hands several times over the next few hundred years. In 1313, whilst the Earl of Moray was in possession, he thoughtfully draped fifty of his enemies' heads on the curtain walls – probably as a public relations exercise. During 1539 there was a determined but unsuccessful assault upon the castle by Donald Gorm of Sleat, who arrived with a fleet of fifty galleys and four hundred clansmen. He was wounded in the leg by an arrow shot by the constable, Duncan MacRae, and in pulling it out, he severed an artery and bled to death.

Eilean Donnan was once taken from the hands of the king's troops by a cunning subterfuge. One of the local farmers asked the governor of the castle for assistance with the harvest, for – as he put it – he knew by the way the ravens croaked that a great storm was brewing. Generously, the governor detailed his garrison to help, but when his troops returned at the end of the day, they discovered the Kintail men in occupation.

The castle was destroyed during the ill-fated Jacobite rising of 1719. The Spanish Government had agreed to synchronise the landing of 5,000 soldiers and arms for 30,000 troops on the west coast of England with the Scottish Jacobite rising. But the intended invasion of England was thwarted by bad weather, as the Spanish Armada from Cadiz encountered violent storms off Finisterre. Only two frigates were able to continue and from these the Earls

◀ *Sgurr an t-Searraich, Kintail, from the old graveyard by the causeway. An easy route to the summit takes the skyline ridge on the right. The mountain is a fine viewpoint.*

Marischal and Seaforth, and Lord George Murray, Marquis of Tullibardine (who was to return again twenty-seven years later with Prince Charlie) and some other officers eventually disembarked with 300 Spanish troops at Eilean Donnan. Though some of Seaforth's men joined them there was trepidation about the ultimate success of the venture, since the abortive 1715 rebellion was still fresh in the minds of the clansmen. Despite this, 1,100 men assembled, most of them bivouacking close to the castle. Some weeks later, three English frigates attacked and re-took the castle and captured the Spanish garrison. The remaining insurgents retreated into the impressive defile of Glen Shiel. Then General Wightman, at the head of the Hanoverian army, advanced on Kintail and on June 9th the battle of the Bridge of Shiel took place. Two hundred Spaniards dug trenches on the slope above the old road, close to the bridge, but didn't give much support to Lord George Murray. When the heather caught fire in the battle, the Jacobite forces had to retreat up the hillside. The peak above the site of the battle is named Sgurr nan Spainteach: the Peak of the Spaniards. After this battle the MacKenzies' lands and titles were forfeited.

In 1932 Eilean Donnan Castle was restored after a work schedule of twenty years' duration and at a cost of £250,000. The castle is open to the public and gives a magnificent, albeit resurrected glimpse into the traumatic and fascinating past.

The Five Sisters of Kintail are lofty ladies but well worth getting to know. Their traverse makes a long, hard day since some 10,000ft of ascent and descent are

◀ *Eilean Donnan Castle, Loch Duich.*

The site of the battle of Shiel Bridge, Kintail. Trenches ▶
were dug in the slopes on the right by Spaniards, who took
part in the battle.

The Five Sisters of Kintail, as seen from Mam Ratagan. ▶ ▶

involved, but escape from the tops, should one tire, is easy. It is better to travel east to west, ascending either by Sgurr na Ciste Dubhe from near the site of the battle, or by the easterly approach to Sgurr nan Spainteach. The last top can be avoided by following the stream down from the final bealach.

The 15,000 acres of Kintail are owned by the National Trust for Scotland and include the Falls of Glomach. These magnificent falls can be reached from several directions. The path up Gleann Choinneachain from beyond Morvich farm offers a longish but rewarding route; it follows the true left of the stream towards the Bealach an Sgairne (Pass of the Murmuring). At one time it was named Cadha Duthac (Narrow Pass of St. Duthac) and his well is to be found at the crest. Remnants of a path slant down northwards into Gleann Gaorsaic, passing Loch a' Bealaich and Loch Gaorsaic. There is no track from here on and frustrating peat hags have to be negotiated from beyond Loch Thuill Easaich (Loch of the Waterfall Hole) to the top of the Falls of Glomach. The other path from Kintail joins in from the left at this point and provides a good way of return after viewing the falls, for it is not so strenuous as the route over St. Duthac's Pass. This path starts from Dorusduain Forestry Commission car park on the north bank of the Abhainn Chonaig and is well sign-

---

◀ *Two approaches to the Falls of Glomach: the far stream, running down from the right, is the Allt a'Ghlomaich and is the route from Bealach an Sgairne; the path in the foreground is the route from Dorsduain. The falls are off to the left.*

En route to the Falls of Glomach from Gleann Gaorsaic. ▶ *The path is seen slanting down from Bealach an Sgairne (right-hand glen), across Loch a'Bealaich.*

Looking up Loch Long on the approach to the Falls of ▶ ▶ *Glomach from the north.*

posted; however, it toils up to 1,700ft, so is not recommended for those suffering from coronary complaints. A third way to the falls, though shorter in mileage, more than makes up for this in squelchy bogs. One must drive first to Ardelve, some miles further west, and cross the confluence of Loch Duich with Loch Alsh. Then take the road following the north shore of Loch Long towards Killilan House whose owner allows motorists to continue as far as Allt a' Ghlomaich, from where a steep 800ft ascent takes one up to the falls. They are well named the Hidden Falls and many tourists are defeated by this aquatic exploration. The head of the falls lies at 1,100ft and from here the Allt a' Ghlomaich plunges 500ft into a deep rocky cauldron. It is the second highest waterfall in Britain, the upper fall alone being 350ft. Care should be exercised, especially in wet weather, on the steep path skirting the falls.

Glenelg:
Iron Age brochs and a road to Skye

BEFORE COMMENCING THE climb over Mam Ratagan, a branch road follows the south-west shore of Loch Duich, passing the snug little village of Letterfearn. Beyond Totaig, at the end of the road, a track leads on towards a gate in a forestry fence. Passing through this gate, a path eventually reaches Caisteal Grugaig, amidst the new forest plantation. This broch has thicker walls than its counterparts in Glenelg and

---

◄ *The Falls of Glomach.*

Looking up Loch Duich from the old road. Mam Ratagan ► *is to the right.*

A short walk beyond Totaig, through a forestry gate, takes ► ► *you to the broch, Caisteal Grugaig. It is reputed to have been originally owned by a woman who had two sons, Trodden and Telve, who owned the Glenelg brochs.*

offers a worthwhile diversion; it looks across Loch Duich towards Eilean Donnan.

The road to Glenelg climbs over the Mam Ratagan Pass (1,116ft) and, once over the bealach, a side road leads off to the right to Kylerhea Ferry. The name is derived from the Fingalian warrior, Riadh, who, according to legend, drowned in an attempt to vault the straits using his spear. It is suggested that Kyle Akin, in Skye, was named after his brother Acunn. Above the ferry, on Glas Bheinn's summit (1,294ft/ 395m), lies an old cairn of the MacCrimmons, the hereditary pipers of the MacLeods of Dunvegan. Here too is Iomaire nam Fear Mor, Ridge of the Big Men. Legend relates that Riadh and other Fingalian heroes are buried here. In 1771 men from the Glenelg district dug up two sarcophagi at this place, containing very large skeletons; one jaw bone was of extraordinary size.

The village of Glenelg lies close to the point where Glen More meets the sea. Nearby are the ruins of Bernera barracks where, from 1722, Hanoverian troops were billeted for seventy years. Gleann Beag is the parallel glen to the south, connected by road to Glenelg. A short way up Gleann Beag are two interesting Iron Age brochs (c.100 BC), Dun Telve and Dun Trodden. Originally their towers would have been forty to fifty foot high. Some five hundred brochs were constructed in Scotland, mostly close to the sea, and in this respect the Gleann Beag brochs are almost unique. It has been suggested that the structures were built as places of refuge during the frequent raids by marauding pirates.

◄ *Kylerhea ferry. Glenelg across the narrows.*

The old Bernera barracks where the Hanoverian troops ►
were billeted for seventy years.

Corran, at the end of the road on the north shore of Loch ► ►
Hourn.

Two southerly sentinels of Gleann Beag are Beinn a' Chapuill (2,421ft/738m) and Beinn Sgritheall (3,196ft/974m), both of which offer fine viewpoints. At the head of the glen the footpath divides. The left-hand branch leads north to Glen More and the Ratagan road. The path that bears south follows the Allt Ghleann Aoidhdailean, then ascends Bealach Aoidhdailean (1,558ft). From the bealach there is no path until Gleann Dubh Lochain is reached. Here, the left-hand route goes on to Kinlochourn, whilst the one to the right runs west to Corran via Dubh Lochain and Glen Arnisdale.

From the west end of Gleann Beag, the road rises to 544ft, then descends to the north shore of Loch Hourn, with Arnisdale and Corran beyond. The road ends at Corran but a path continues along the shore to Caolas Mor and it is from this path that the great north-east corrie of Ladhar Bheinn in Knoydart is best viewed. There is a daily post boat from Arnisdale to Barrisdale, and a daily bus service from Arnisdale to Glenelg.

◄ *Dun Telve from Dun Trodden, Glenelg. Iron Age brochs which were probably built about the time of the Roman occupation in Scotland.*

Gaelic and Norse Glossary

A	river, stream; terminally: -a, e.g. Calda (*kalda*), cold stream; gen: ar, e.g. Aros (*ar-oss*), river's mouth. (Norse).
Aber, Abar,	also as: Obar, mouth or confluence of a river.
Abhainn,	usually Avon, river.
Amhainn	
Achadh	usually Ach, field, park.
Ailean	a green place; plain.
Airidh	sheiling.
Aisir	a rocky defile or pass.
Allt	also as: Ald, Alt, Auld, Ault, burn, brook, stream.
Aoineadh	a steep promontory or brae.
Aonach	a height, a ridge.
Ard, Aird	a high point, promontory.
Ath	a ford, also a kiln.
Ay, Ey, I	island, e.g. Pabbay, priest's island; Rona, rough island; Handa, sand island (Norse).
Baile	usually Bal, Bali, town, homestead.
Bàn	white, fair.
Bàrr	a point, extremity.
Bàrd	a poet, a dyke, enclosure, ward.
Beag	also as: Beg, little, small.
Bealach	breach, pass, gap, col.
Beinn	also as: Ben, a mountain.
Beithe	a birch tree.
Bian	a hide (of cattle).
Bidean	summit, e.g. Bidean Druim nan Ramh, summit of the ridge of oars.
Binnean	also as: Binnein, a pinnacle or little mountain.
Blàr	a plain, battlefield.
Bò (pl. Bà)	cow, cows.
Bodach	an old man, hobgoblin, spectre.
Ból	farm, abode, e.g. Ullapool, Ulli's farm; Resipol. (Norse).
Borg	fort, e.g. Boreraig, fort bay. (Norse).
Bost	township, e.g. Kirkabost, church town.(Norse).
Both	also as: Bothan, a hut, booth or bothy.
Bràigh	usually Brae, Bread, top, summit.
Brekka	a slope, e.g. Clibrick, cliff. (Norse).
Bròg	a shoe.
Bruaich	a bank, brae, brim, steep place.
Buachaille	a herdsman.
Buidhe	yellow, golden coloured.
Cadh	a pass, steep path.
Cailleach	a nun, old woman, a witch.
Caisteal	castle, e.g. Caisteal Uisdean, Hugh's castle.
Cam	crooked, bent, one-eyed.
Camas	also as: Camus, bay, bend, channel.
Caol	also as: Caolas, Kyle, strait, firth, narrow.
Càrn	a heap of stones, cairn.
Carr	broken ground.
Ceann	also as: Ken, Kin, head, headland, e.g. Ceann na Beinn, head of the mountain.

Cill, Kil	a cell, church.
Cioch	a pap, woman's breast, e.g. Sgurr na Ciche, peak of the pap.
Clach	a stone.
Clachan	stones, hamlet.
Cladh	a churchyard, a burying place.
Clais	a hollow.
Cleit	a ridge, reef; rocky eminence.
Cnap	a knob, hillock.
Cnoc, Knock	a knoll.
Coill, Coille	a wood, forest.
Coire	Anglicised form: Corrie, a cauldron, kettle, circular hollow.
Corran	a sickle; semi-circular bay.
Creag	also as: Craig, a rock, cliff, e.g. Creag an Iolaire, eagle's rock
Crioch	boundary, frontier, landmark.
Crò	a sheep-fold, pen.
Crom	bent, sloping, crooked.
Cruach	stack, heap, haunch.
Cuinneag	a milking pail or stoup, e.g. Quinag, from its shape.
Cùl	the back.
Ciùe	nook.
Dail	a field. Cf. Dalr, e.g. Armadale, bay dale; Bracadale, slope dale; Arnisdale, Arni's dale. (Norse).
Dearg	red.
Doire	grove, hollow.
Druim	also as: Drem, Drom, Drum, the back, ridge.
Dobhar	water, a stream, e.g. Morar, great water.
Dorus	door. Deoch an doruis, a stirrup-cup.
Dubh, Dhu	black, dark.
Dùn	a fort, castle, heap.
Eagach	notched.
Eala	a swan.
Ear	east.
Eas	a waterfall.
Easach	a cascade.
Easg	bog, fen, natural ditch.
Eilean	an island.
Eyrr	gravelly bank or beach, e.g. Erradale, gravel beach dale.
Fada	long. e.g. Beinn Fhada, long mountain.
Fas, Fasadh	a stance, a firm spot, e.g. Fassiefern, the alder stance.
Feadan	narrow glen.
Fearn	an alder tree.
Féith	bog, sinewy stream, a vein.
Fiadh	a deer.
Fionn	fair, white, e.g. Fionaven, the White Ben.
Fjall	hill, fell, e.g. Helaval, flagstone fell. (Norse).
Fjord	firth, e.g. Snizort, Sni's firth or snow firth; Ainort, Einor's firth; Sunart (Suaineort), Svein's bay. (Norse).
Fuaran	a perennial spring, well.
Gabhar	a goat.

Garbh, Garve	rough, e.g. Garbh Bheinn, rough, wild mountain.
Geal	white, clear, bright.
Geodha	a narrow creek, chasm, rift, cove.
Gearanach	a wall-like ridge.
Geàrr	short.
Gil	cleft, e.g. Idrigil, outer cleft. (Norse).
Glais	a stream, burn.
Glas	grey, pale, wan, green.
Glac	a hollow, dell, defile.
Gleann	usually Glen, narrow valley, dale, dell.
Gob	point, beak.
Gorm	blue, azure, green.
Gualann	shoulder of mountain or hill.
Inbhir	also as: Inver, confluence of river and sea.
Iubhair	yew tree.
Lag	usually Lagan, Logie, a hollow in a hill.
Lair	an axe.
Lairig	the sloping face of a hill, a pass.
Leac	a ledge, e.g. Leac na Fionn, the bright ledge.
Leathad	a slope, declivity.
Leathan	broad.
Leitir	a slope.
Liath	grey.
Linne	pool, sound, channel.
Lòn	a marsh, morass.
Lùb	a bend, fold, curvature.
Màm	a round or gently rising hill.
Maol	headland, bald top, cape.
Meall	knob, lump, rounded hill.
Monadh	moor, heath, hill, mountain.
Mòine	also as: Mointeach, peat-mossland, mossy
Mór	great, large, tall. Anglicised form: More.
Muc	a pig, e.g. Eilean nam Muc, Isle of Muck.
Muileann	mill.
Muir	the sea.
Mullach	a rounded hill.
Nes	nose, point, promontory, e.g. Waternish, water ness; Duirinish, deer ness; Greshornish, pig ness. (Norse).
Odhar	dapple, drab, dun-coloured, sallow.
Ord	a round, steep, or conical hill.
Os	outlet of a lake or river. C.f. Oss, river mouth. (Norse).
Pit, Pet	farm, hollow.
Poll	pool, pond, pit.
Rathad	a road, way.
Réidh	plain, level, smooth.
Riabhach	also as: Riach, drab, greyish, brindled, grizzled.
Righ	king

Roinn	a point, headland, peninsula.
Ros, Ross	a point, promontory.
Roth	wheel of cart, halo.
Ruadh	red, reddish.
Rudha	usually Ru, Rhu, Row, promontory.
Ruighe	also as: Righe, a forearm, cattle run, slope, sheiling.

Sean	old, aged, ancient.
Setr	a sheiling, e.g. Marishader, mare's sheiling. (Norse).
Sgorr, Sgurr, Scaur	a peak, conical sharp rock, e.g. Sgurr nan Gillean, peak of the young lads.
Sgreamach	rocky.
Sìth	a fairy. Sìthean, a fairy hillock or knoll.
Sker	skerry, isolated sea rock, e.g. Sulasgeir, pillar skerry. (Norse).
Slettr	smooth, e.g. Slattadale, smooth dale. (Norse).
Slige	a shell, e.g. Sligachan, a shelly place.
Slochd	a deep hollow.
Sneachd	snow.
Socach	snout.
Srath, Strath	a wide valley, plain beside a river.
Sròn, Strone	nose, peak, promontory.
Sruth, Struan	a stream, current.
Stac	a steep rock, conical hill. (Norse).
Stadr	steading, e.g. Conista, lady's steading; Monkstadt, monk's steading. (Norse).
Stafr	staff, post, e.g. Staffa (*stafr-ey*), pillar isle.(Norse).
Staurr	a stake, pillar. (Norse).
Stob	a point.
Stùc	a pinnacle, peak, conical steep rock.
Suidhe	sitting, resting place.

Tairbeart	also as: Tarbert, Tarbet, an isthmus.
Taigh, Tigh	usually Tay, Ty, a house.
Teallach	a forge.
Tìr, Tyr	country, region, land.
Tobar	a well, spring, fountain.
Toll	a hole.
Tom	a hillock, mound.
Tòrr	a mound, heap, hill.
Tulach	knoll, hillock, eminence. Anglicised forms: Tilly, Tully, Tulloch.

Uachdar	usually Auchter, Ochter, upper land.
Uaine	green.
Uamh	a cave, grave.
Uchd	ascent, face of a hill.
Uig	a nook, bay.
Uisge	water, rain.

Vagr	a bay, e.g. Stornaway (*stjornarvagr*), rudder bay. (Norse).
Vatn	water, lake. Common in Lewis, e.g.Sandwood (*sandabhat*), sandy water or loch. (Norse).

INDEX

Map references are given in italic, pictures in **bold** *type*

A

Abhainn Chonaig, *244–5*, 233
Abhain Rath, *86–7*, 92
A' Chailleach, 45
A' Chill, *192*, 193
Achallader, 64
Acharacle, *129*, 131, 141, 143
Achintee, *86–7*, 97
Achnacarry, 183
Achnambeithach, *48*
Achnanellan, *129*, 141
Achtriochtan farm, 53, 67
Affric Lodge, *210*, 219
Affric, River, *210*
Ainshval, *192*
Aline, River, 121
Allt a' Chailleach, 24, *32–3*
Allt a' Ghlomaich, *224–5*, **232**, 237
Allt a' Mhuillin, *86–7*, **100**, 101, 105
Allt Ghleann Aoidhdailean, *224–5*, 245
Allt na Muidhe, *32–3*
Allt na Ruigh, *32–3*
Altnafeadh, *32–3*, 39, **40**, **41**
Am Bodach, *32–3*
An Cruachan, *192*, 208
An Sgurr, see Sgurr of Eigg
An Stac, **154**
An t-Sron, *32–3*, *48*, 53, 57, **58**, 61, **62**
Aonach Beag, *86–7*, 95, **96**, **111**
Aonach Dubh, *32–3*, 43, **47**, **48**, 49, **50**, **51**, 53, 57, **58**, **62**
Aonach Eagach 43, 45, **46**, **47**
Aonach Mor, *86–7*, 95, **96**
Appin, 77, 81, **83**, 84, 121
Ardelve, *224–5*, 237
Ardgour, **72**, 113
Ardnamurchan, 113, 128–43, *129*, **130**, **136**, **137**, **140**, **142**; Point, *129*, 139, 143
Ardnish, *156–7*, 159
Ardtoe, *129*, 143
Ardtornish, 119, *120*; Bay, *120*, 127, 128; Castle, *120*, 123, **125**, 126, 127, 128; Point, *120*, 126
Arisaig, 149, **150**, 153, *156–7*, 159, 164
Armadale, *156–7*
Arnisdale, 175, *224–5*, 245
Askival, *192*, 197

B

Ba Bridge; River, *22–3*; Cottage, 20, *22–3*
Ballachulish, *32–3*, *48*, 74, 75, 77, **78**, **80**, 82; Bridge, 35, 81
Banavie, 183, 185
Barcaldine, 65
Barrisdale, *156–7*, 175, 245
Bay of the Spaniards, 128, 135
Bealach an Sgairne, *224–5*, 233, **234**
   Aoidhdailean, *224–5*, 245
   Dearg, *32–3*, *48*, **50**, 53, **54**, **55**, 57
   Feith 'n Amean, *113*, **115**, 117
   Fhionnghail, *32–3*, 61
Beinn a' Bheithir, 74, 75, **76**, **78**, **79**, **80**
   a' Chapuill, *224–5*, 245
   Airein, *192*, 193
   Bhan, 75, 77
   Bhuidhe, *192*, 208
   Dorain, 19
   Fhada, *32–3*, *48*, 49, **50**, 53
   Maol Chaluim, *32–3*, 61
   Resipol, 199, *120*, 128, *129*, 131, **132**, 141
   Sgritheall, *224–5*, 245
Ben Hiant, *129*, 131, **138**, 139
   Lui, *16*, **17**, **18**
   Nevis, 35, 43, *86–7*, **90**, **93**, 97, **98–101**, **103–107**, **110**, **111**, **184**, **185**
   Starav, 35
Bernera barracks, *224–5*, 241, **242**
Bidean Coire, *32–3*, *48*, 49, 53, 57, **58**, 61
Bidean nam Bian, *32–3*, *48*, 49, 53, **55**, 57, **58**, **59**, 61, **62**, **82**
Binnein Mor, *86–7*, 89
Black Corries, *22–3*, 24
Black Mount, 20
Blackwater Reservoir, 43, *86–7*
Black Wood of Rannoch, 20
Borrodale, River, *156–7*, **158**, 159
Bracora, *156–7*, 165
Bracorina, *156–7*, 165
Bridge of Orchy, *16*, 19, *22–3*, 24, 64
Brinacory Island, *156–7*, **166**, **168**
Brunery, *129*, 149
Buachaille Etive Beag, 39, **42**, 43
Buachaille Etive Mor, **30**, 31, *32–3*, **34**, 35, **36**, **37**, **38**, 39, **40**

C

Caisteal Grugaig, *224–5*, 237, **239**
Caisteal na Gruagaich, 119, 120, 121,
  122
Caledon, Forest of, 20
Caledonian Canal, 209, *210*
Callert, *86–7*, 89
Camas nan Geall, *129*, **130**, 131
Camas Sciotaig, *192*, 208
Camusrory, *156–7*, 169, 175, 187
Canna, Isle of, 135, *192*, 193, **194**,
  200
Cannich, *210*, 219
Caol Creran, *32–3*, 63
Caolas Mor, *156–7*, 223, *224–5*, 245
Cape Wrath, 16
Carn a' Ghaill, *192*, 193
Carna Island, *120*, 123, *129*, 131
Carnach, River, *156–7*, 175, 187
Carn Beag Dearg, 101
Carn Mor Dearg, *86–7*, **90**, **99**, **100**,
  101, **102**, **103**, 105, **106**
Carnoch, **70**; River, *113*, 117
Castle Stalker, 74, **75**, 77, 81, **83**, 84
Castle Tioram, *129*, 143, **144**
Cathedral Cave, *192*, 205, **207**, 208
Cave of Francis, *192*, 205, 208
Clach Leathad, 20, *22–3*, 24, 27, **28**
Clad Chiarain, *129*, **130**, 131, **133**,
  134
Cleadale, *192*, 208
Coe, River, *32–3*, *48*, **51**, 53, 61
Coire a' Chothruim, 117
  an Easain, 27
  an Iubhair, *113*, **115**, **116**, 117,
    119
  an Lochain, *86–7*, 89
  Cloiche Finne, *32–3*, 39
  Gabhail, *32–3*, 48, 49, **50**, **51**,
    53, **54**, **55**, 57, 66
  Gaothach, *16*, 19
  Leis, *86–7*, **103**, 105
  na Tulaich, *32–3*, 35, 39
  nam Beith, *48*, 49, 57
  nan Lochan, *32–3*, *48*, 53, 57
  Ruigh, *32–3*, 45
Coireach a' Ba, **28**
Commando Memorial, **186**
Compass Hill, *192*, 193
Cononish, River, 16, 19
Corran, *224–5*, **243**, 245
Corran ferry, 113 **114**, *120*
Corrieyairack Pass, 94, *210*, 214
Corrour, *108*, 109
Cuil Bay, 84
Coupall, River, *32–3*, 35

Crowberry gully, 37, **37**; ridge, 31,
  35, **37**; tower, 31, **38**
Cruachan, 35
Cuillin, 35; (Rhum), **136**, **198–9**

D

Dalelia, *129*, 141, 145, 149, **150**, 153
Dalness, *32–3*
Dark Mile, 183
Dessary, River, *156–7*, 191
Devil's Staircase, *32–3*, **41**, 43, 45,
  89
Dibidal, *192*, 197
Doire Asamaidh, *156–7*, 175
Dorusdain, 233
Druim an Iubhair, 113, 117
Dubh Lochain, *156–7*, 175
Dun Ban, *192*, 193
    Telve, *224–5*, 241, **244**
    Todden, *224–5*, 241

E

Eigg, Island of, **136**, 143, **148**, *192*,
  201–*8*, **206**, 223
Eilean Donnan, 223, *224–5*, 227,
  228, 229, 241
    Fhionnan, *129*, 149, **150**, 151,
      152
    Munde, **60**, **70**
    nan Gobhar, *129*, 153
Etive, River, *22–3*

F

Falls of Glomach, *224–5*, 233, **236**,
  237
Fasnakyle, *210*, 219
Fillan Bridge, *16*; River, 19
Fionn Ghleann, *32–3*
Five Sisters of Kintail, 224–5, 229,
  231, 233
Forest Lodge, 20, **21**, *22–3*, **28**
Fort Augustus, 94, *210*, 211, **213**,
  214, 217
Fort William, 65, 67, 84, *86–7*, 89,
  92, 95, 97

G

Garbh Bheinn, 35, **72**, *113*, **115**,
  116, 117, 119
Gearr Aonach, *32–3*, *48*, 49, **50**, **51**,
  56
Glas Bheinn, *224–5*, 241
Glass, River, *210*, 219
Gleann a' Chaolais, 75, 77

Gleann a' Chaorainn, *156–7*, **190**, 191
  an Dubh Lochain, *156–7*, 175, **178**, 180
  Beag, *224–4*, 241, 245
  Cia-aig, 183
  Choinneachain, *224–5*, 233
  Dubh Lochain, *224–5*, 245
  Gaorsaic, *224–5*, 233, **234**
  Geal, *120*, 121
  -leac-na-muidhe, *32–3*, 48, 61, 63, **68**, 69
  Medail, *156–7*, 175, **180**, 187
  na Guiserein, *156–7*, 179
  Righ, *86–7*, 89
Glen Affric, 210, 219, **220**
  Arnisdale, *224–5*, 245
  Barrisdale, *156–7*
  Borrodale, *156–7*, 159, 164; House, **160**, 163
  Creran, 63, *75*, 77
  Dessary, *156–7*, 187, **189**, **190**, 191
  Duror, *75*, 77
  Etive, 20, *22–3*, 27, 31, *32–3*, 39, **44**, 63
  Finnan, *156–7*
  Gour, *120*, 128
  Kinglass, 19, *22–3*
  More, *224–5*, 241, 245
  Moriston, *210*
  Nevis, 84, *86–7*, 89, **90**, **91**, 92, 95, **107**
  Pean, *156–7*, **190**, 191
  Roy, *108*, 109, **112**
  Salachan, *75*
  Shiel, *210*, *224–5*, 229
  Sligachan, 15, 77
  Spean, 94, *108*, 109
  Tarbert, *113*, **116**, 117, 119, *120*
  Urquhart, *210*, 215
Glenaladale, *129*, 153
Glenborrodale, *129*, 131, 145
Glencoe, 20, 24, **25**, **30**, 31–74, *32–3*, **34**, **36**, **41**, **46**, *48*, **52**, **55**, **58**, **59**, **60**, **62**, **82**
Glenelg, *224–5*, 237–45, **240**
Glenetive Forest, *32–3*, 61
Glenfinnan, *156–7*, 179, **182**, 191
Glensanda, 119, *120*, 121, **122**
Glenuig Bay, *129*, 153
Gorteneorn farm, *75*, 77
Gortenfern, *129*, 141
Gour, River, 113, 128
Great Everite, 128, 139, **140**
Great Glen, 209, *210*

H
Hallival, *192*, 197
Harris (Rhum), *192*, 195, 197, **198**

I
Innean a' Cheathaich (the Anvil or Study, Glencoe), 45, 49
Inveraray, 65, 84
Invercharnan, *32–3*
Invercoe, 63, **68**, 69
Invergarry, *210*, 211, **212**, 219
Inverie, *156–7*, 169, 171, 175, **177**, 179
Inverlochy Castle, *86–7*, 92, **93**, 94, 95, 211, 215
Invermoriston, *210*
Inveroran, *22–3*
Inverrigan, 69, 73
Inversanda House, *113*, 119

K
Keil, 84
Kentallen, 84
Kenra Bay, *129*, 141, 142
Kilchoan, *129*, 131, **136**, **138**, 139, 141
Killilan House, *224–5*, 237
Kilmory (Ardnamurchan), *129*, 141
Kilmory (Rhum), *192*, 197
Kingairloch, 117, 119, *120*, 121
Kingshouse Hotel, 20, *22–3*, 24, **26**, 27, 29, **30**, 31, 35, 45
Kinloch, *192*, 195, **196**, 197
Kinlochailort, **155**
Kinlochaline Castle, *120*, 123, *124*, 126
Kinlocharkaig, *156–7*, 191
Kinlochleven, *32–3*, 43, 84, **85**, *86–7*, 89, 95, 109
Kinlochmoidart, *129*, 145, **146**
Kinlochourn, *156–7*, 175, *210*, 219, 223, *224–5*, 245
Kintail, 223–37, *224–5*
Knoydart, *156–7*, 171, **176**, 187
Kyle of Lochalsh, 8, 169
Kyle Rhea, 169, *224–5*
Kyleknoydart, **174**
Kylerhea, *224–5*, **240**, 241

L
Ladhar Bheinn, *156–7*, 179, **222**, 223, 245
Lagangarbh, *32–3*, 35, **40**

Lairig Eilde, *32–3*, *39*, 48
Lairig Gartain, *32–3*, 39, **41**, **44**
Lairig Leacach, *86–7*, 89, 108, 109
Lairigmor, *86–7*, 89
Larachbeg, *120*, 123
Laroch, River, *75*, 77
Laudale House, **118**, 119, *120*
Leanachan Forest, 95
Letterfearn, *224–5*, 237
Loch a' Bealaich, *224–5*, 233, **234**
　　a' Choire, 119, *120*
　Achtriochtan, *32–3*, 48, 57
　Affric, 20, *210*, 218
　Ailort, *129*, 153, 159
　Aline, *120*, 123, 126
　Alsh, 223, *224–5*, 237
　Arienas, *120*, 121
　Arkaig, *156–7*, 169, 183, 187,
　　188, **190**, 191
　Ba, *22–3*, 24
　Beinn a' Mheadhoin, *210*, 219,
　　220
　Cluanie, *210*, 219
　Dochard, 20, *22–3*
　Duich, *210*, 223, *224–5*, 237,
　　238
　Dunalastair, 20
　Eil, *86–7*, *156–7*, **184**
　Eilde Beag, *86–7*, 89
　Eilde Mor, 84, *86–7*, 89
　Eilt, *156–7*
　Ericht, 20
　Etive, 20, *22–3*
　Gaorsaic, *224–5*, 233
　Garry, *210*, 219, **221**
　Hourn, *156–7*, 171, 175, *210*,
　　222, 223, **243**, 245
　Laich, *75*, 77
　Laidon, *22–3*, 24
　Leven, 57, 67, **68**, *75*, **76**, **85**,
　　86–7, **88**, 89
　Linnhe, *75*, *86–7*, 113, 117,
　　119, *120*, 121, 209
　Lochy, 209, *210*
　Long, 223, *224–5*, **235**, 237
　Loyne, *210*
　Moidart, *129*, 143, **148**, 149, 153
　Morar, *156–7*, 164, 165, **166**,
　　167, **168**, 169, 171, 191, 217
　nan Cilltean, *156–7*, 164
　nan Uamh, *156–7*, **158**, 159,
　　163, 164
　Ness, 8, 165, 209, *210*, 215–19
　Nevis, *156–7*, 165, 169, 171
　　173, **174**, 175, **176**, 187, **189**
　Oich, 209, **210**, 211

Ossian, *86–7*, 97, *108*, 109, **110**,
　　111
Quoich, *156–7*, *210*, 219
Rannoch, 20
Scresort, *192*, 195
Shiel, 119, *129*, 141, 149, **150**,
　　153, *156–7*, **181**, **182**, 183
Sunart, 117, **118**, 119, *120*, 123,
　　128, 131, **132**
Teacuis, 119, *120*, 121, 131
Thuill Easaich, *224–5*, 233
Treig, *86–7*, 89, 97, *108*, 109
Tulla, *22–3*, 24
Tummel, 20
Lochaber, 24
Lochailort, **154**
Lochaline, 119, *120*, 121, 123, 126
Lochan a' Chuirn Duibh, *156–7*,
　　165
　a' Mhaim, **189**
　Lunn Da-Bhra, *86–7*, 89
　Meall an t-Suidhe, 97, 105
　na Fola, *32–3*, 39, **42**, 43, 45
　nam Breac, *156–7*, 175
　Stole, *156–7*, 165
Luibeilt, *86–7*, 89, 92, 97, *108*, 109
Luinne Bheinn, *156–7*, 175

M
Mallaig, *156–7*, 165, 169, **170**, 171,
　　172, 175, 183
Mallaigmore, *156–7*, 169
Mallaigvaig, *156–7*, 169
Mam Barrisdale, *156–7*, 175
　Meadail, *156–7*, 175
　na Cloich' Airde, *156–7*, 187,
　　189
　Ratagan, *224–5*, 237, **238**, 241
　Uidhe, 179
Marmore Lodge, *86–7*, **88**, 89
Marmores, 35, 43, 57, **80**, 84, *86–7*,
　　88, 89, 92, **102**, **107**
Meall a' Bhuiridh, 20, *22–3*, 24, **25**,
　　26, 27, **28**
Meall an t-Suidhe, *86–7*, 97
Meall Bhuidhe, *156–7*, 175
Meal Sanna, 139, **140**
Meeting of the Three Waters, *32–3*,
　　48, 49
Mingary Castle, *129*, 131, 135, **137**
Moidart, 113, *129*, **144**, 145, 153;
　　Seven Men of, 145, **147**
Morar, *156–7*, **161**, 164; River, 164
Morvern, 113, 119, *120*, 127;
　　Witches, 128

Morvich farm, *224–5*, 233
Muck, Isle of, 135, *192*, 193–5
Mull, Isle of, **125**, *129*, 135, 139;
    Sound of, *120*, 126

N
Nevis, River, 97
North Ballachulish, *86–7*

O
Oban, *16*
Oban, (L. Morar), *156–7*, 191
Ockle, *129*, 141
Onich, *86–7*, 89
Oronsay Island, *120*, 123, *129*, 131
Ossian's Shower Bath, 61

P
Pap of Glencoe, *32–3*, 45, **60**, 61, **80**,
    88
Parallel Roads, *108*, 109, **112**
Pean, River, *156–7*, 191
Polloch, 128 *129*, 183
Port na Cairidh, 139
Port nan Spainteach, *129*, 135
Portnacroish, 81
Portree, 14, 15
Portuairk, *129*, 139
Prince Charlie's Cave, *156–7*
Prince's Beach, *156–7*, **158**, 159;
    Cairn, **162**

R
Rahoy, *120*, 121, 123
Rannoch Moor, 8, 9, 20, *22–3*, 24,
    27, 35, **37**, 43
Red Burn, 97, 105
Rhum, Isle of, **136**, 143, *192*,
    195–201, **196–200**, **203**
Road to the Isles, 109
Rois Bheinn, *129*, 153, **154**, **155**
Roshven, *129*, 153
Roybridge, *108*, 109
Rubh' Ard Ghamhsgail, 159

S
Salen, *120*, *129*, 131
Sallachan, *120*, 128
Samalaman Bay, *129*, 153
Sanday, Isle of, *192*, 193
Sanna Bay, *129*, 139, **140**

Schiehallion, 35
Scotstown, *120*, 128
Sgorr Bhan, 77
    Dhearg, 74, 75, 77
    Dhonuill, 74, 75, 77
    na h-Ulaidh, *32–3*
Sgurr an t-Searraich, **226**
    Coire Choineachain, **177**
    Fhuaran, *224–5*
    na Carnach, *224–5*
    na Ciche, *156–7*, 171, **174**, **180**,
        187
    na Ciste Dubhe, *224–5*, 233
    na Moràich, *224–5*
    nan Gillean (Rhum), *192*
    nan Saighead, *224–5*
    nan Spainteach, *224–5*, 233
    of Eigg, *192*, 201, **202–4**, 208
Shiel Bridge, *129*, 143, *224–5*, **230**;
    River, 143, *224–5*
Skye, Isle of, 14, 164, 169
Sleat, Sound of, *156–7*, 164
Small Isles, 169, *192*, 193–208
Smearisary, *129*, 153
Sourlies, *156–7*, 187
South Tarbet, *156–7*, 165
Spean Bridge, *86–7*, 89, 92, *108*,
    109, 183
Sron a' Gharbh, *113*, **115**, **116**, 117
    na Creise, **26**, 27, 31
Steall, cottage, *86–7*, **90**; Lower, 92;
    Upper, 92, 95; waterfall **91**, 92
Stob a' Ghlais Choire, **26**, 27
    Coire Altruim, *32–3*, 39
    Coire nam Beith, *32–3*, *48*, 49,
        58, 61, **62**
    Dearg, 31, 39, **40**
    Dubh, *32–3*, 39, **44**
    Ghabhair, 20, *22–3*, **28**
    Mhic Mhartuim, *32–3*, 45
    na Broige, *32–3*, 39, **44**
    na Doire, *32–3*, 39
    nan Cobar, *32–3*, 39
    nan Lochan, *48*, 49, 53, **55**, **56**,
        57, **58**, **62**
Stoul, *156–7*, 165
Strathan, *156–7*, 187, 191
Streap, **190**
Strontian, **118**, *120*, 128, *129*, 183
Sunart, *120*, 128, *129*
Swordle, *129*, 139

T
Tarbert, River, *113*
Tabet, *156–7*, 165, 169, 171, **173**

Three Sisters of Glencoe, see
 Aonach Dubh, Beinn Fhada,
 Gearr Aonach
Tobermory, *129*, 135, 139
Tor a' Bhalbhain, *156–7*
Torlundy, *86–7*, 105
Totaig, *224–5*, 237
Tyndrum, 8, *16*, **17**, **18**

U
Urquhart Castle, *210*, 215, **216**, 217, 219

W
Water of Nevis, *86–7*, 92
West Laroch, 77
White Corries chairlift, **34**